Pooh Sticks in the Gutter

The Chronicles of a War Baby

BARBARA COOP

ISIS
LARGE PRINT
Oxford

First published in Great Britain 2004
by Isis Publishing Ltd.

Published in Large Print 2004 by ISIS Publishing Ltd,
7 Centremead, Osney Mead, Oxford OX2 0ES
by arrangement with the author

British Library Cataloguing in Publication Data
Coop, Barbara
   Pooh sticks in the gutter: chronicles of a war baby.
   – Large print ed. – (Isis reminiscence series)
   1. Coop, Barbara – Childhood and youth
   2. Coop, Barbara – Homes and haunts – England
   – Bolton
   3. Large type books
   4. Bolton (England) – Social life and customs
   – 20th century
   5. Bolton (England) – Biography
   I. Title
   942.7'37085'092

ISBN 0–7531–9942–4 (hb)
ISBN 0–7531–9943–2 (pb)

Printed and bound by Antony Rowe, Chippenham

Contents

Introduction

The year 2001 seemed to be a bit of a watershed in my life. I had made up my mind to retire, and found myself with time to think about the future. A phone call one day, when I was up a ladder painting a window, brought me down to earth with a sharp thud.

My twin sister Jean had been involved in a road accident and lay in a critical condition in intensive care. All her limbs were shattered. She was given a scant 40 per cent chance of survival, and lay barely conscious for weeks. Her recovery was slow and painful, and I found myself thinking of the close life we had shared as children, and about the later years when we had drifted slowly apart as we each travelled our separate ways. As she lay unconscious, I made a conscious effort to will my strength to her, not knowing if the link we had closely shared was broken in the passage of time. She did survive; with or without my strength we will never know.

This is the story of our childhood in the years following the Second World War in a very different England to the one we now know.

CHAPTER ONE

Beginnings

Life has always been a shared experience, in my case even more so. Being born a twin during the Second World War, I found the rationing included divided attention from Mum and an absence of our father for the duration. Luckily for us a loving Granny and Grandad gave us a happy and caring start.

We were born in July 1944, first Jean, impatient as always, weighing a scant four pounds, and me a half hour later as an unexpected bonus, weighing in at four and a half. Shock followed. In the days before scans and the excellent ante-natal care given nowadays, childbirth was a bit of a hit and miss affair. Twins were something of a novelty, especially if they were identical, and we were like two peas in a pod. Mum rose to instant celebrity overnight, and Grandma was sent to buy an extra set of everything, to kit out the extra new arrival. In the small village on the outskirts of Leeds, everyone knew everyone else and their business, and Mum's early delivery caused a bit of excitement for a day or so, then the war news took over again.

Babies were after all commonplace, but not to Mum. Life was never to be the same for Mum again, with two babies to see to, who demanded her instantaneous attention, both at the same time, and with no husband to help. Dad never did see us as new-borns. When he came home, we were toddlers in our siren suits, wondering who this strange sunburned man was, and why he was the cause of so much fuss.

Mum lived with Granny and Grandad in a two-up two-down terraced house on a steep hill. It had a cellar and an attic, and a shared outside privy. It was also rented.

Dad had volunteered at the outbreak of the war and gone into the catering corps, spending some time in France, being promoted to Company Sergeant Major in charge of feeding a battalion of soldiers. After Dunkirk they were married, and shortly after Dad left for India and Burma via Suez. His few and far-between leaves were spent in this little house with her.

To him it was all a big adventure, and he was never to settle down again in his home village. His wanderlust, being hard to subdue, finally faded away in Bolton in Lancashire, no doubt washed away by the seemingly endless rain I remember from my childhood.

Granny was a godsend. Anyone who has had twins will know the dilemma of which to see to first. We were two halves of the same. We sat one at each end of the big rickety second-hand pram. Sometimes in desperation we were sat back to back so we couldn't see one another, Mum declaring we had a conspiracy and that if we couldn't see one another, we couldn't communicate. It didn't work. One cried when the other cried, and each stopped feeding when the other did. If one was feverish, so was the other, and through it all we laughed and gurgled to one another. That is when we weren't crying. Poor Mum, but thank God for Granny, and think what Dad missed!

We lived with Granny and long-suffering Grandad for two years and then, after V.J. Day Dad arrived home. Mum, Granny and especially Grandad must have been overjoyed to see him. We weren't so sure. Every time he loomed over us we burst into tears, and it took some time for us to get accustomed to him. I'm sure he must have felt the same. Finally we all declared a truce and became a family at last. The next job was to find us a home. After all, we couldn't expect to live with Granny and long-suffering Grandad in - their small rented terraced house for ever. Dad went to see his old boss at the bakery, hoping to get his old job back. But things had moved on while he was away, new lads had been trained, and he had been supplanted by a youth who had been a lad when he went away to war. No Job, No Home, No Money.

Dad struck out with most of the local jobs. Like most Demobs, who had arrived home well after V.E. Day, he was late home and caught out. Work in bakeries was limited owing to rationing being in force. He wasn't qualified for much else; he had started work as an apprentice at the age of fourteen and instantly loved the job, in spite of the early start at four a.m. His ambition outweighed his financial situation, for one day he intended to have his own shop. Right now he needed a job to finance his ambition and, with a wife and two toddlers to feed, life in Horsforth looked bleak to say the least.

5

Dad's parents were higher up the social scale than Mum's. Grandad Toothill had a tailoring business. Most of his antecedents were tailors, owing to their beginnings in Leeds, a clothing manufacturing city. Grandad's two sisters were well-known costumiers and dressmakers in the Leeds district of Armley. Both spinsters, their marriage prospects had diminished in the shortage of suitors caused by the slaughter of the First World War. Grace and Alice lived at home, neither ever managing to flee the nest, one dying in her early forties from a ruptured appendix after years of corresponding with her young man, an Australian soldier who had served in France and had eventually returned home after tiring of begging her to return with him.

The two sisters and two brothers ran their tailoring business from their home in a terraced street in Armley. Grace and Alice made ladies' costumes and dresses, and Grandad Toothill and brother Harry haberdashery and suits for the well-attired. A third sibling, Joe, was gassed in the First World War. I remember him as an old man gasping for breath and wearing bottle-top glasses whose grip on his nose turned it a bluish shade of purple. As a lad he had rebelled, refusing to join the family business, and he became an ostler looking after the local brewery dray horses. His love and devotion to them was not returned when an accident involving them and a runaway dray wagon left him with severely injured feet from which he never really recovered. He was left with a limp and a healthy respect for his charges, but it never lessened his great love for them, and in time he returned once more to care for them until he was too old and no longer able to do so.

As a child I remember Joe and Grace in their dotage. We would visit them in their old fashioned kitchen, where we all sat around the table, a cup of tea served in their best china resting on the red chenille tablecloth that had a fringe of bobbles around it. Some were missing. The talk was over our heads, gossip mostly, and when we began to fidget Mum would send us outside where we found a fatal fascination in the old tippler toilet, which had a rough wooden seat with two holes, side by side. The parlour was only used at Christmas, when a visit would entail sitting perfectly still for an hour or more on the faded bottle green chaise-longue, until Auntie Grace let us play with the old treadle sewing machine, which stood in the corner covered in dust.

All the walls had pictures of cows in fields or drinking by the side of lakes. Heavy faded green curtains blocked out most of the natural light, but the aspidistra on the big round pedestal table seemed to thrive, for it was enormous. Dad would tell us of their father, who had died in the bedroom upstairs of dropsy, and of how, when he died, his dead body had burst, and all the water had run through the floorboards and into the parlour below. Mum would laugh and say it must have fed the aspidistra. It was always something she commented on when it was brought up. Family joke or not, we always looked for stains on the musty old carpet square when we were allowed in there. Auntie Grace and Uncle Joe lived together in that house in Simpson Grove until death parted them, well into their eighties. Neither married, content in each other's company until the end. Harry and Albert took wives. Harry married Nan, a Scottish lass he met on holiday, and went eventually to live in Glasgow. They had a son, their only child, young Harry who died in childhood which was a great source of sadness to them. Albert, Grandad Toothill, married May, whose maiden name was Flower. We always laughed at that for Dad said it was her proper name — Mayflower Toothill.

They had a daughter, Vera, and Dad, who arrived four years later, and set up tailoring from their home at Sunnybank Road in Horsforth. Their business thrived, enabling them to buy a car, which in those days put them in the higher income bracket. Both children attended Leeds Grammar school, and they owned their own home, no mean feat in the 1920s and 1930s. Respect was due.

Mum and Grandma never got on. It was very civilised, but Mum spoke her own mind. She called it sticking up for herself, and tact was somewhat low on her list of attributes, as was knowing when to keep her mouth firmly shut. It didn't make her many friends. The trouble was Mum was never good enough for Sonny (Dad was christened Cyril, but to the family, he was always Sonny). Sonny by name and sunny by nature. You could say Mum came from the other side of the tracks. Grandad Handford was a printer by trade, and he worked for the local advertiser in Horsforth, a family firm employing a number of people. Joe was one of twelve brothers, a quite common size of family in the nineteenth century.

Granny Handford was a local lass, who looked after her father and younger brother. Her mother was an invalid. Part of Grandad's life was spent in South Africa fighting the Boers, and he also served in India, where he became very fond of cricket. Mum was born in 1915, but he didn't see her until she was four years old. She was a sickly child, and very small for her age. Sickly and thin as she was, Granny managed to rear her, and she is still going strong today at the ripe old age of 88. Mum's sister Auntie Phyllis was born four years earlier in 1911. Grandad returned to England in 1919, and never left these shores again. At the outbreak of the Second World War he was too old to fight, but was called to rally to the aid of the local cricket team, left short of players by the war. Devoted once more to his beloved cricket, Saturdays were spent, when the weather was agreeable, in Horsforth Hall Park, family in tow to cheer him on. It was a regular family pastime, not to be missed.

Granny Handford, my favourite Granny, was lovely. She had twinkling eyes and a hearty laugh. Her life as a child had been harder than most. Her father was a strict Methodist and a disciplinarian, and anyone straying from the straight and narrow was severely punished with a strap. She had to do all the housework, no mean feat in those days of coal fires, look after an invalid mother, and care for a younger brother from a very early age. All this as well as working in a factory in Leeds, sewing buttons on shirts. One hot day, after work she went swimming with a friend in a local pond. After enquiring why her waist length hair was wet, he flew into a temper, and in his rage took the scissors to it as a punishment. He was a very cruel man and Granny was very afraid of him. Joe Handford carried her away from one life of poverty to another.

They lived in a two-up two-down rented terraced house in Rose Avenue, one of several lines of terraces on a steep hill. It had an attic, a cellar, a small yard with a patch of grass, and an outside privy shared by the next door neighbour. They used to take it in turns to stock it with cut sheets of newspaper, hung on a piece of string attached to a bent nail. It was full of spiders, had a small frosted glass window, and a tongue and groove door, which just missed the toilet seat when it was opened. The door had a latch handle, and a piece of string to fasten to a hook to keep it private when in use, and a large gap at the bottom, through which the wind would whistle with a vengeance in winter. All the Mod Cons for the age. There was some discussion as to whether or not it should be whitewashed at one time, but the upkeep of this was debatable, agreement couldn't be reached, so it never was.

The cellar was divided into two as was the custom. One side was the coal hole where the coalman tipped two bags a week through a grating in the yard. The other was the posh part, divided from the coal hole by a brick wall and a door with a latch. The posh part was whitewashed. There were shelves along one wall and a stone ledge. On the other wall, the tin bath, posser, washboard, peg bag and washing line lived side by side.

On the stone ledge a large earthenware urn covered with a tea towel took pride of place. This was Granny's bread crock, constantly replenished with fresh home made cottage loaves and bloomers. She baked every other day to keep it topped up. On the shelves were jars of fruit, chutneys, honey and a butter safe with jugs of milk covered by nets to keep out any livestock. It had a flagged floor and was always freezing.

A spiral stone staircase led down into the cellar from the kitchen above, the edges of the steps of which were donkey stoned. The cellar had a smell of its own but that of whitewash predominated. The cellar was scrubbed once a week and the steps re-donkey stoned, the donkey stone being acquired from the rag and bone man in exchange for old worn-out clothes which couldn't be patched any more. If the cellar had livestock, it wasn't Granny's fault; the mouse traps were attended to with gusto, each success a great source of satisfaction. Granny was an avid baker and tins of all shapes and sizes held cakes of all varieties that she could knock up from the rations.

Seed cake, a fatless variety, was one of the favourites, and, more important, cheap to make. Jam pastry was another. Two layers of pastry with a smear of raspberry jam between, the edges turned over and pricked with a fork, and the whole baked in the oven for half an hour. She always had a batch for us when we visited, and when we came to stay for any length of time she was kept busy baking it in vast quantities, with both of us stood on a chair either side of her at the kitchen table, each possessed of a fork to stab at it to make the holes before it was put into the oven.

We all lived in Granny's house when Dad came back: us, Mum, Dad, Granny and Grandad. Grandma Toothill's house was posher and she had nice nick-nacks, but Mum wouldn't live there, and I don't think we were welcome to. Mum had "pinched" Sonny and Grandma Toothill couldn't and wouldn't forget. We would go to visit but it was always a bit of a dull occasion, as we had to sit still and she didn't make a fuss of us as Granny did. Once the new gossip had been passed on and the family news glossed over, the small talk ran out, and Dad was itching to be off. We would be half carried and half walked down Stanhope Drive from Grandma's house and along New Road Side and return to Granny's lovely homely abode, which we called home.

Grandma Toothill's house stood at the end of a long front garden. The stone wall which contained it was of rough limestone, encrusted with moss and yellow spots of lichen. The gate opened on to a long path of crazy paving down the edge of a long smooth manicured lawn, kept in weekly trim by an ancient gardener, who trundled an old lawnmower up and down for what seemed like hours. It was extremely neat with flower borders all round containing endless Michaelmas daisies, which seemed to suit Grandma's personality, sort of dull and quiet and rather mauve.

The back of the house was very much a different kettle of fish. It was like a jungle, lots of weeds, tall grass at least a foot high, with a path of flattened grass leading to the dustbin and coal bunker. Further down was a bed of strawberries, creeping out onto a bank at the end. I don't think the gardener ever ventured there, only to tip the weekly grass cuttings from the front lawn into a pile at the back of the coal bunker, which by the end of summer formed a huge pile for the field mice to snuggle up in.

The garden was like Grandma, posh on the outside, but the bits you didn't see were rather dull. However, it put Granny's pocket handkerchief lawn and snapdragons to shame. Grandma Toothill's house, being at the posh end of town, unlike Granny's had a box bay window in which to display her aspidistra, by then way out of fashion. But it held pride of place there in an otherwise boring parlour.

Grandma's parlour, which she didn't keep for visitors only, was full of heavy mahogany furniture. A large sideboard dominated one wall, displaying a chiming clock which rang out the quarter hour and chimed on the hour, disturbing the quietness that always pervaded the place. A pair of Dresden shepherdesses stood either side under glass domes in an attempt to keep out the dust from the coal fire, which burned even in summer. A horsehair sofa and armchairs crowded around the fireplace, and more ornaments adorned the mantelpiece, high out of reach of our inquisitive hands. Various pictures hung from the picture rail, half eclipsing the faded, once glorious, wallpapered walls. Like Auntie Grace's, they were of grazing cows and sheep, unlikely to draw attention from the faded square of red carpet that hugged the centre of the room. Once luxurious and colourful, it now vied for attention with the dark brown floorboards that edged the room.

Grandma Toothill's parlour and Granny's cellar were the two rooms I remember most vividly from my childhood. Both instilled in me a faint chill, the "I don't know what's lurking" feeling of the cellar, and the "Don't touch that" parlour of Grandma where we were obliged to be seen and not heard, as children of her day were. When I think of those days and our visits to the Grandmas, I see Granny Handford in her cellar fetching coal, putting away the baking, just "doing" and Grandma Toothill sitting by her fireside in the posh parlour, legs agape, in front of her coal fire, deep in thought with her thick lisle stockings all wrinkly around the ankles.

Grandad Toothill was a shadowy figure in our lives. I remember very little of him, and he died very early in our lives, in his late 60s, of hardening of the arteries, no doubt caused, with today's hindsight, by a sedentary job and the Yorkshire high fat diet of a reasonably wealthy man, not to mention the lack of exercise, due in part to early car ownership. Grandma and Grandad Toothill seemed old, although they can't have been much older than their early 60s just after the war. He always wore a well-tailored suit with a waistcoat and a pocket watch on a thick gold chain and, when he went out, he donned a trilby and woollen overcoat to suit his status in life. Like his brother Joe, he wore thick bottle-top glasses.

He was shorter than Grandma, which seemed to give him a henpecked appearance but, according to Mum, he was kind and very much a ladies' man, choosing to flatter rather than criticise, a trait that led to a notoriety for a certain fondness for the ladies, if not actually being a Romeo. My most vivid memory of him was of going to tea one day, with my sister and my two younger cousins, Auntie Vera's daughters, and sitting around the tea table when it collapsed. All the cakes, sandwiches, and the teacups and saucers slid to the floor with an almighty crash. Grandma screamed and we youngsters burst into floods of tears. After comforting us with a few soothing words after the initial shock, Grandad cleared up the mess, salvaging what he could of the tea, while Grandma took us into the parlour, out of the way.

We all laughed about it afterwards, but what a fuss! It remains my strongest memory of him, for shortly afterwards he died. Grandma lived on another twenty years without her Albert and, on better acquaintance, a certain wry dry humour emerged, which no doubt carried her through to acceptance of her widowhood, one of life's bitter blows. Mum was brought up, along with her sister, as a strict Methodist or, as Dad called them, Wesley thieves. Chapel played a big part in her early life. Not that she was particularly religious, though certainly a believer in the Day of Judgement when we will all be called on to account for our black marks in the big book, and in the theory that He was always watching, writing it down to be answered for when we got to those big gates in heaven. We were often threatened when we misbehaved, "He's watching, writing it all down," a threat to make us think twice before we carried on, wondering if it was worth a black mark or not.

Mum's main interest in church was the social activities it provided, and the active social life it gave her. It was there she met and made her friends and joined a circle of young people out to have fun. In a world before television, everyone made their own entertainment. Money was by no means plentiful, more often in short supply, but it didn't seem to matter much. Walking was free and the countryside was nearby. Mum played tennis and every free moment found her and her tennis chums on the tennis courts in Horsforth Hall Park. Church socials were frequent and the pictures were regular and cheap. Quite good-looking, with fair hair finger-waved in the current style, and very fashion conscious, she had lots of boyfriends.

Mary, Mum's best friend, had the same sense of humour, and both were "fast". Mary's family were poor and her mother begged and borrowed to get them through life. Mary, likewise pushy and cheeky, snapped up the best of the boyfriends, so Mum soon learned to stand her ground. Between them, they acquired a no-nonsense reputation, but they were popular and stylish. Mum worked in Guiseley, and travelled there every day by bus or bicycle, or sometimes shank's pony. She was employed by the Phillips factory, putting filaments into light bulbs, a job which required a steady hand. During the war she worked long hours. In the blackout and winter, the journey to and from work was sometimes rather difficult. Weekends were for fun and usually included the Saturday night dance at Broadway Hall.

Ballroom dancing was one of Mum's favourite pastimes and the big bands were in full swing. Glen Miller was her particular favourite. She met Dad for the first time at one of these dances, but at the time he was currently squiring her sister Phyllis, eventually asking her out when Phyllis ditched him for Tom, a van driver who was a talented artist and whom she eventually married. They too lived with Granny and Grandad until they found a small terraced house to rent in the next street. After the war and another rented house, they bought their small cosy home, and lived out their lives there, interspaced with holidays in Whitby and the Lake District, where Uncle Tom painted the local beauty spots and Whitby's picturesque harbour. They were a devoted couple, and their one great sadness was being unable to have children, which must have left a great gap in their lives.

Auntie Phyllis devoted a lot of her time to the small garden that edged her home. She was particularly fond of the cottage garden variety of flowers, and stocks and snapdragons vied for space among the sweet peas, while her favourite carnations, in deep pinks and vibrant reds, grew in great clumps along the stone walls, coated in profusion with Tumbling Teds and aubrietias. Sea pinks in great cushions clung perilously to the limestone and mortar walls, bobbing in the wind. The old-fashioned simple cottage garden she tended, kneeling in her cross-over pinafore with slippers and Uncle Tom's socks on her feet.

Dad's sister, Auntie Vera, was our only other close blood-relative. Older than Dad, "our Vee" as she was always called, had a close and loving relationship with Mum and Dad. When we all moved away to Blackpool and then Bolton, Auntie Vee's letters kept us close. Her newsy letters arrived regularly, full of family news and local gossip. When Dad acquired a car in 1949, we all piled happily into it for the two-hour journey to Horsforth to see them all — Grandmas, Grandads, Aunties, Uncles, one and all — for the short time we were able to stay.

First we would call at Victoria Gardens to see Auntie Phyllis and Uncle Tom, then on to Granny and Grandad's in Rose Avenue, where we were greeted with lots of hugs and smothered in kisses, in time for a Sunday lunch of roast beef and Yorkshire pudding, served the old way with the pudding first course, and the meat and vegetables to follow, with Granny's special gravy, made with Oxo cubes, something Mum didn't use. We always had a sponge pudding too, which we never got at home because Mum never had time to make one, with the shop and all. Lunch, which was called dinner in Yorkshire, was then cleared away, with us all helping to wash the pots, while Dad and Grandad folded the table down and put it away, back in its place in the window. We stayed then until all the gossip was chewed over, and Grandad and Dad had finished their snooze, an integral part of the proceedings, but typical of men.

Then the goodbyes and more hugs and kisses followed as we all piled back in the car once more to move on to Grandma and Grandad Toothill's, where Dad wouldn't dare to fall asleep, and we would be expected to sit still for the whole length of the visit. After Grandad Toothill had died, Grandma was usually to be found at Auntie Vee's on a Sunday, so we were spared the whole of that visit thankfully. I think Mum was glad, too, because she didn't have to keep shushing us when we made the effort to join in too boisterously. Finally it was on to Auntie Vee and Uncle Laurence's in Broadgate Drive. Running down the path to the back door where we always entered with a knock and a loud "Cooeee!", what fun those visits were, how we all laughed, what noise the eight of us must have made, as we exchanged news and gossip once more, and Uncle Laurence fixed us kids up with a game of Snakes and Ladders to keep us amused. Auntie Vee and Uncle Laurence lived on a council estate, a two-bedroomed house with a through living room.

It was the most homely house I have ever been in, with a coal fire and a warmth of family feeling rarely come across today. Rag rugs made by Auntie Vee and Grandma covered the kitchen floor, and the rest of the rooms I remember, as well. The garden I never remember as being very tidy. There was a stretch of grass and a garage, with a large sprawl of strawberries that we would raid in summer when there were any, as we played on the swing at the bottom of the garden. Susan and Ann were three and four years younger than us, respectively, and seemed to live on a diet of frequent biscuits between meals, which were often left because they were "picky eaters". Sometimes Auntie Vee would do her utmost to get them to eat and often in vain fill them up with biscuits, to ease between-meal hunger pangs, which had them hanging around her pinafore, constantly begging for more.

There would always be a treat for us, whenever we went. Something she had made, a pretty smocked dress each, or a jumper. She was a very talented needlewoman, something Mum seldom had the time or inclination to be. We always had tea at their house, and played a game, Mum and Dad too, until it was that horrible time to go home. Always begging for a bit longer, we would eventually be rounded up and secured in the back seat of the old Morris 12, with a travelling rug over us to keep us warm if we fell asleep, to trundle back over the Pennines to Bolton and the rain. Many was the time we had to stop to let Mum out for some fresh air or to be sick, something she called a bilious attack. She was always quiet after they had discussed all the freshly gained gossip. I think she was feeling sad at leaving all her relatives, because there was always a dash to the toilet and often a few tears when we got home, and we were always sent straight to bed with a cup of hot milk and the excuse "school tomorrow, come on". We were sad too, and Uncle Laurence would race the car to the end of the street with Susan and Ann, waving like mad as we turned the corner and out of their lives once again.

These were our relatives, all we had, and they were all on the other side of the Pennines. Susan and Ann would make fun of our "Lankie" accent when we got older. We copied our school friends' accent, then they wouldn't mock our Yorkshire one, so we ended up with a half and half one eventually.

CHAPTER
TWO

Blackpool

After the war, when Dad had come home, he had some difficulty in settling down again. Life with a wife and two young daughters in chilly England was very different from his life as a soldier in tropical Burma. Glad as he was that he had come through the war unscathed, the future must have looked pretty mundane after his experiences abroad. He still kept in contact with his old army pals, scattered as they were through the country. One obviously having the same problem of settling down again contacted him with a proposition to go out to Kenya to start up a bakery with him. Despite the apparently good prospects of the job, Mum was concerned as to our welfare, feeling we were too young to take all the way to Kenya, and that the risk to our health was just too great. Granny wasn't too keen either, as she would lose Mum as well as us.

If Mum hadn't had us, they most likely would have gone, but what with malaria and the other tropical diseases to consider, and medicine not being what it is now, and Granny's opposition, it just wasn't an option. Dad was disappointed, but having considered the risks involved, decided to try his luck in Blackpool, where he managed to land a job in a bakers and confectioners. To start with Dad went on his own, and found lodgings. It wasn't much use moving us all lock stock and barrel if the job didn't work out, so he was gone a few weeks before finding his feet and deciding whether or not to stay. One of the problems in Horsforth was the situation between Mum and Grandma, who just didn't want to let go of "Her Sonny" who Mum had "pinched".

For years after they had left, Mum had to take the flak for dragging him away to Blackpool, Grandma not believing it was Dad who wanted to get away to cut the apron strings that he found once again bound him to Grandma. As in all families there was some acrimony on both sides with each side blaming the other, and it must have come as a great relief when it was time for us to actually pack up and go. It must have been with great regret for Granny, and a great relief to Grandad, when Dad finally came to get us all to start our new life in Blackpool, and wave goodbye to what must have been a difficult situation.

At first we lived, or should I say lodged, with Mr. and Mrs. Shepherd, who I vaguely remember made a great fuss of us as two year olds, and was very kind to Mum when Dad was working extremely long hours away from us. We didn't live with them long, and Dad soon found us a nice if somewhat small house to live in. It was in Preston Old Road, Marton, on the outskirts of Blackpool. My vague memories of the place at two years old paint a very spartan place, with linoleum floors which Mum managed to tart up with a few of Auntie Vera's and Grandma's old but bright rag rugs. It seemed to have very little furniture, but as the place was rented I think it must have been ready furnished, and with old mis-matched stuff in dark wood which gave the rooms a gloomy look.

We slept in a cot at first, in a room of our own, and I remember the thrill of feeling grown up when Mum moved us to a bed, on which she piled lots of blankets tucked in to stop us falling out. One night, we had a tremendous storm, with loud thunder and lightning. I remember us screaming for Mum; it was dark but for the lightning flashing into the room. After that we were afraid of the dark, despite Mum's insistence that it was only Santa Claus dropping his sack — a likely story, but one she stuck to come what may. In later years, when we were at Auntie Phyllis's, any hint of thunder and lightning would find us all scurrying for cover to the cupboard under the stairs or, if we were at Granny's, into the cellar until it finished. Auntie Phyllis was as terrified of thunderstorms as we were. We eventually grew out of it, but she had no such excuse, and remained scared, still hiding under the stairs at the first crack of thunder, much to our amusement in later years.

Our playmate in Blackpool was Muriel. She was six and talked with a lisp. We all played in the back street, which was covered in cinders from everyone's ash pit, not very knee-friendly to two year olds. There were a lot of scraped knees, plasters and tears, and we were also afraid of dogs. The very appearance of one in the back street sent us into screams of hysteria, which in turn brought Mum flying out thinking we were badly hurt, only to have us spring up into her arms and around her neck, out of reach of the poor inquisitive creature, who only wanted to play.

Despite the dogs, playing in the back street was fun as Muriel would put us in her old doll's pram and pretend we were her babies. One day we disappeared and Mum was in a panic. Eventually we turned up as Mum and Muriel's Mum searched for us, Muriel wheeling the pram, very non-plussed, with both of us piled into it. We all got told off for leaving the back street, and Muriel was in disgrace. We were dragged inside and made to sit still, while they lectured us on the evils of bad men who gathered up lost children and took them away. After that, we were very wary of men, wondering if they were the bad ones who took children away. I suppose it was one way of keeping us in the back street where bad men didn't lurk very often.

In those days there was very little traffic, so we weren't really in danger of being knocked down, especially as we were a good way off the main road. We were bought little tricycles to play on, very tinny in red. I suppose at the time they were good toys, but by today's standard they were dangerous, with sharp edges, and very flimsy. Mum always seemed to be picking us up, and dusting us down after they had toppled over. Mr. and Mrs. Shepherd, who we had all lodged with when we first came to Blackpool, came to see us and take us for walks to give Mum a break now and again. They were in their 60s, and I suppose they were substitute Grandparents for a while, although they never came to see us when we moved to Bolton.

They would take us to the cemetery across the road, and we would help Mr. Shepherd tidy up the gravestones, some of which were very overgrown. It was a virtual wilderness, with sky-high grass at times, and we would play hide and seek in the grass, with them pretending not to be able to see us. Then Mrs. Shepherd would get out her flask, and pour him a cup of tea, using the flat gravestone slabs for a table top, not very reverent, but I suppose necessary. We often spent the afternoon in here, jumping on the gravestones and off again, not very reverent either but then we didn't know any better at two. Mrs. Shepherd would read the inscriptions to us in a sing-song voice and then it was time to go home, to Mum, who would ask us if we had had a nice time.

I have very distinct memories of that cemetery, and so has my sister Jean. In fact, whenever we go to Blackpool, that cemetery invokes a strong pull as we go through Marton, and I strain my head to see it as we go past. It still looks the same, and I wonder if Mr. and Mrs. Shepherd, who tended to the graves and picnicked with the dead, are tended to as well. If they lie there, I hope that their graves are not jumped on by two little girls who don't know any better.

Mum would often take us across the fields to the shops. If it was lunchtime we would stop at the local school to watch the children playing in the school yard. None of them wore a school uniform; there wouldn't have been the money for them in those days. We would watch them through the flat railings, being careful not to stick our heads through as one day we watched a little boy get his head stuck, and the fire brigade had to be called to get him out. Mum was very careful to remind us of his fate and the grease they had to put on his head to get him free as he screamed blue murder. Sometimes she would lift us over to play with Muriel and her friends, while she chatted to some of the other Mum s, and the teacher came out to ring the handbell and line the children up, and then file them back into school on the ring of the second bell.

Sometimes, when the weather was fit, we would go to the promenade, and look at the tower and the sea, and get on a tram to ride up to Bispham and back again, getting off where we got on, just for the thrill of it, and to see the sea.

Dad worked long hours. I don't remember him being there a lot of the time, and when he came home we were put to bed after him kissing us goodnight, but we could hear them laughing and chatting before we fell asleep. We were always co-conspirators and quite mischievous as toddlers. One day, exploring where we shouldn't, we found some red pills. Jean had climbed on a chair and managed to open a drawer in the sideboard. Thinking they were sweets she gave me some, but they were very bitter and I spat them out. Jean, thinking they were Smarties swallowed several. Later she was very sick. I remember vividly Mum shaking me, shouting and asking what we had eaten. I said we had found some Smarties in the sideboard, and was very frightened and crying because Mum was so cross. They were iron pills and Jean was taken to Blackpool Royal Infirmary, where she was kept in. She

26

was away for what seemed a long time, and Granny came to stay, while Mum went to see her every day.

Living in Blackpool, we found ourselves very popular with Mum and Dad's friends and relatives alike, so we had lots of visitors to stay, especially in the summer when no sooner had one lot gone home than another lot took their place. Mum enjoyed the company, especially Auntie Vera and Uncle Laurence, whose new baby, Susan Elizabeth, would be taken into the downstairs guest bedroom to feed, while Mum ushered us out of the way. We were always curious as to why she didn't have her tea at the table like us, and found her quite fascinating even if she couldn't yet play like we did.

Dad worked even longer hours in summer, when we hardly ever saw him, something that would eventually lead to a decision to find a better way of life. When he was home, he would take each of us in turn on the crossbar of his bike down to the paper shop, which made us squeal with delight, despite the discomfort. The rest of the time we played with Muriel in the back street. Toys were few, and apart from the little tricycles and Muriel's old pram, we would play with anything at hand which gave us amusement. The toilets at the end of the street proved a great attraction, and we played with the bright shiny brass knobs on the doors. Finding one part open one day, we all three went inside and the door shut on us, locking us all in. After ten minutes or so of screaming, we were let out by a kind lady who came to investigate the noise, taking us home to Mum with tear-streaked faces where we received no sympathy. Nevertheless it taught us a lesson we would not forget, and gave Mum and Dad great amusement.

The field next to the cemetery also held some fascination, despite it being across the road we were forbidden to cross. Two horses were kept in it, and it was fenced with rails and posts. One day we slipped under the rails to get a better look. As the two curious horses galloped towards us, we fled screaming and Muriel pulled us back under the fence. It wasn't the first time we had come into contact with them either, for they chased us as we crossed the field one day on a short cut to the shops, Mum dragging us as we all ran and literally throwing us over the fence at the other side. After that we stayed away from them.

It was not so simple with dogs, though. We were terrified, especially if we didn't know them. The mere approach of a dog sent shivers of fear into us. Mum later told us that, when we were babies, a dog had jumped at the pram, tipping it over. After that, we only had to see a dog for the sight to set us off screaming, and no amount of reasoning would pacify us until the dog had disappeared. Even now in my fifties, a strange dog approaching has me nervously teetering on the edge of crossing the road. Only the silliness of it makes me hold my ground, offering a friendly "Hello, doggy" to it in the hope that it won't bite me.

Winters in Blackpool were bitter, bleak and cold. When the wind came off the sea, no matter how many clothes we had on it found its way to us, nipping our fingers and toes despite our mittens and woollen socks. Mum bought us red "siren suits" with fur on the hoods, and, when we had grown out of these, woollen coats and leggings and bonnets with pom-poms on top. Even so we always had coughs and colds. Bracing Blackpool, they called it — it certainly was when we lived there. Occasionally a week was spent in Horsforth with Granny. Dad would put us, all three, on the train with a suitcase, and we would be met at the other end by Grandad and Granny in Leeds, Grandad to carry the suitcase and Granny to carry one of us home to the little house in Rose Avenue we had once called home. Summer being the busy season, Dad couldn't be spared and unfortunately had to stay at home.

Our days were spent, once we had settled in, visiting all our relatives who we didn't see very often. When the days were fine and warm, we would go to the park. At weekends we would watch Grandad play cricket which usually accounted for Saturdays and on Sunday, after Granny had been to chapel, we would go home to our Sunday lunch, and then on to the park again, to cheer him on if he was batting. He loved his cricket, and despite being in his sixties he played well too.

Mum would take us to see her old friends, and there would be a lot of laughing and going back over old times, as well as catching up on all the gossip she had missed by being away. Days out were spent at Yeadon Dam, taking the bus and a picnic. Other days were spent at Roundhay Park in Leeds where we played on the swings, and tried to find our way out of the maze. Then we caught the bus back past Kirkstall Abbey to the bottom of Granny's street, to drag tired little legs up the hill and through the back gate into Granny's kitchen where the kettle was put on straight away to revive us all. Rationing was still in force, so sweets were a special treat, requiring one of the special coupons Mum and Granny carried in their purses. Even so we were allotted a certain amount during the week. Grandad, now retired, took us into the print works where he used to work to show us off, and we, in awe, would stand there quietly while various people came to look at us, until shyness overcame us and we clung to Grandad, hiding behind him, while they laughed at our faces, all pink and bashful.

Life in those days after the war seemed comparatively simple compared to life today. Meals were simple and filling, usually a bit of meat and two veg. if you were lucky, not much variety and never foreign foods. Sweets were always sold from jars, weighed on a little scale which had a brass receptacle to hold them until they were poured into a small paper cornet bag and exchanged for your money. Entertainment was usually pictures or, if you hadn't any money, the wireless. It was also a very unhurried pace of life, and it wasn't often you saw someone dashing off somewhere in a hurry, with no time for anything, like we do today. Mostly if people were unhappy with their lot there wasn't much they could do about it, only work harder and try to save what little they could for a rainy day.

Granny listened to the wireless and was an ardent fan of *Mrs Dale's Diary* and *The Archers* until the day she died. They were the equivalent of today's soaps. Other times were spent drinking cups of tea in the houses of neighbours, with whom she became good friends, some of whom Mum grew up with, their children almost becoming Mum and Auntie Phyllis's siblings, they were so close. Granny's special friend was Mrs. Husselby, who lived next door but one down. Clifford Husselby was Mum's "honorary brother" for years, their exploits becoming legendary in our family. The families were friends and neighbours for forty years, until Mrs. Husselby went to live near her daughter in Thorne, near Doncaster, when they needed one another the most to fill the gap left by their deceased husbands.

Mum and Dad stayed in Blackpool for two years. Much of that time Mum was on her own, coping with two toddlers and rather lonely. Dad was working most of the time, and when he was home he was catching up with sleep. Mum would take us down to the beach or the prom when the weather allowed. He kept in contact with his old army mates, and sometimes with their families they came to stay for a few days in summer, when the house seemed never to be empty. When one lot went, another lot took their place, or so it seemed. Except in winter, when Mum needed them most. It was the winter desolation that eventually made them decide to leave. Blackpool was one of the premier destinations of its day, popular with mill-workers on their Wakes Week holiday, when entire towns would close down and mass evacuation would take place to the seaside for those who had managed to put enough money into the "Didlum Fund", run by some enterprising soul, who was entitled to take a percentage of it when it was paid out. This was often a risky business for some, who often found the fund holder had blown the cash and had disappeared when pay-out time arrived.

Mum would take us down to the station to meet the train if someone was coming to stay with us. The train doors would fly open as the train came to a stop, and people with suitcases and paper parcels and carriers spilled out on to the platform in great numbers, groups of young men and girls eyeing each other up and eager to get the fun started, shouting to one another over the din. There were families loaded up with suitcases, kids in tow trundling battered tin buckets and rusty spades, kept in hope from the previous year, Mums and Dads harassed and excited at the same time, trying to keep track of kids and belongings in the mêlée, as they flooded off the platform in the hurry to get to their digs and have a cup of tea.

Dad, after two years in Blackpool, decided to move on. He wanted to open his own business, and set about looking for a premises with potential. He didn't want to stay in Blackpool because of the desolation in winter and the cold wind which swept in to fill us with coughs and colds, one after the other. Neither did he want to return to Horsforth and Grandma's apron strings. He set out to find a shop with living accommodation, the shop having to have all-round good trade, and his search took him all round the mill towns of the north west, to Blackburn, Bury, Oldham and the cotton towns on the edge of the Pennines. Finally he decided on a little shop in Bolton, roughly half way between Blackpool and Leeds. Situated twelve miles from Manchester, Bolton was a cotton manufacturing town;

now like all the rest its mills have been demolished or taken over by various businesses to use as cash and carry warehouses or furniture showrooms. To leave Bolton involves a climb, for every road out of the town is uphill. Situated in a bowl on the moors, Bolton takes its name from that fact. It has a good thrice weekly outdoor market, a Victorian market hall of some character, and a very ornate Victorian town hall, set in the centre of a spacious square. At one time there was a good engineering industry, and a whole flurry of cotton mills set up to weave the cotton which came to Liverpool from America in the nineteenth century. Most people know it from its football team, "The Wanderers", a team to be reckoned with when Nat Lofthouse kicked a ball about for us and was known as "The Lion of Vienna". Dad's shop was in Derby Street, one of the many streets leading out of the town. It was surrounded on all sides by mills, shops, public houses, cinemas and terraced streets of poor quality houses, built at the time of the Industrial Revolution or just after to house the workers that flocked from the country to work in the mills. Dad decided it had the makings of a "little gold mine", even if the living quarters behind and above were not much to be written home about. The shop was nicely fitted out with mahogany counters and marble window-shelving and slabs for cooling and displaying bread and cakes. There was a living room behind and a small scullery which passed for a kitchen, a yard complete with outside privy and, attached by a long passage covered by a tin roof to keep out the rain, a bakehouse, with a rough concrete floor, which must have been tacked on in what was once a long yard.

This was the worst of the place. The walls were brick with umpteen layers of white lime-wash at various peeling stages, which was rectified at intervals by bashing to loosen the larger flakes and re-lime washing. It was a regular sight, when we were growing up, to see Dad in old clothes, scarf and thick hairnet, and a pair of old glasses, covered in white lime, sloshing the burning stuff on to the walls in a haphazard way, at the top of a ladder, balancing the tin of lime against his chest, and hoping he wouldn't fall off the ten feet or so on to the concrete floor. Once, however, a visit to the hospital was called for when lime got into Mum's eye. It was red for days, and was a lesson to them both as she suffered from the burning agony of it. After that Dad invested in a pair of swimming goggles, which completed his comical outfit for the job, giving the local bobbies many a laugh when they called in for a cup of tea and a chat over the back door, which they did often.

Two bedrooms, each with a fireplace, and a bathroom of sorts, although it didn't contain a toilet, just a bath and a washbasin, and a large airing cupboard containing the water tank, completed the property. As property went in the 1940s, it met the standards. Mum and Dad packed us off to live with Granny and Grandad while they moved in and sorted things out. Utility furniture was bought locally second-hand, and the dark asphalt floor was covered in a square of bright red coconut matting. The living room had an open fire with a back boiler to heat the water, mysteriously operated by a damper which Mum seemed to be eternally pulling up and down. A rack for drying clothes was positioned over it; probably today it would be regarded as a fire hazard, but then it was essential to dry our clothes in winter.

The small kitchen was a sorry affair, comprising a stone sink supported on two brick pillars with a piece of string threaded through a curtain hiding the slops bucket into which, among other things, the tea leaves were thrown, and a gas stove standing on legs. A kitchenette, a tall cupboard and drawer concoction, with a flap which dropped down to make a table and worktop, took up pride of place on the end wall, and tins of food, pots and pans and all the kitchen odds and ends took up residence here, the hub of the kitchen. Mum was very proud of it, for it was the latest of Mod. Cons. in the age before fitted kitchens. Ours was a sickly shade of yellow, and had frosted glass doors and chrome handles, soon to bubble in the damp atmosphere. It lasted for years as things did in those days, despite being rather wobbly and top heavy when the flap was down. Over the years the hinges became rather strained, and things had a tendency to slide off. Many a meal or snack was dusted down, and slammed back on to a plate over the years, with us being none the wiser.

The outside privy backed on to the coal shed where we kept the house-fire coal, next to the kitchen. Infested with spiders, it too was lime-washed and flaking. An overhead tank with chain and wooden handle dripped with cobwebs, and there was no light.

Mum had to stand at the door in winter when it was dark, both of us being afraid of the livestock that lurked within. Many a large spider scuttled off at the sound of a piercing shriek. An old plank door with a "sneck" the only lock sufficed to keep out the rain. A six-inch gap, while allowing in the local cats hunting for spiders and mice, ensured a healthy ventilation which in the winter turned into a penetrating draft. None of us lingered longer than necessary, even though Dad sometimes took in the newspaper to read, leading to it being re-christened the reading room by Mum. On exiting, he would venture into what we called "The Coke Hole", to stoke up the oven in which he baked his bread and muffins, and pause a while to thaw out after his "sojourn to The Reading Room". This covered part of the yard was to prove a popular place to us kids and cats alike in wet weather. It provided a warm and fascinating place in which to play. We never gave a thought to it being dangerous as it proved to be to Jean when she was scalded badly on the arm while we were making "tea" for our dolls in one of our games.

In winter all who ventured to the privy would be found with hands spread palms down in front of the "stoke hole" door, thawing out in ecstatic pleasure before they hurried in through the yard and up the passage to heave open the heavy old plank door into the draughty living room. They'd be greeted by a chorus of "put wood in t'ole", while Mum, who felt the cold acutely, and still does to this day, would block up the gap under the door in a futile attempt to keep out the cold. A huge keyhole from an earlier lock served as a peephole until Dad stuck a bit of bread dough into it, effective for a while until it turned green with mould, when it would be poked out and replaced with a fresh piece.

Mum and Dad left us with Granny for six weeks. In that time they learned quickly how to run their business, and became accustomed to their new home and surroundings. We settled down with Granny again and, as children do, ceased to miss our parents. It was a shock, therefore, when Granny and Grandad packed up our things. Not that we had much, just the usual "one on, one in the wash, and Sunday best" that most people had in the years following the war. We set off to catch the train in thick fog, only to find either we had missed it or it was not running. Anyway, we returned home again and Grandad was sent to telephone through to say we were not coming, and Granny took off our coats, bonnets and leggings. The next day we tried again, this time more successfully. I remember the fog more than I remember the train journey the next day, of which I remember nothing at all, only being hugged by Mum and Dad on arrival at our new home, Mum crying and lifting us up on the sideboard to take off our coats and leggings. She couldn't stop hugging us.

The bakehouse made a big impression. We were taken down a long passage that seemed endless, and shown the dough mixer in which Dad mixed his bread and the dough cutter which cut it into pieces to be moulded into flour cakes, and had to be swung on by Dad. This was later to become one of our playthings, as we swung around the handle, doing "Tipple-Overs" when it was too wet to play outside. We were shown the big black oven with two shiny doors, which Dad opened to show us the heat it contained and to warn us of its danger; not that we could reach to open the doors if we wanted to. It stretched way above our heads and six or seven feet into the wall, and was lined in brick and stone which never went cold, stoked constantly with coke to keep up the heat. The ceiling stretched endlessly above us, and a washing line, hung with several pairs of socks, dangled high above the oven, waving in the heat.

We must have been very small, Jean and I, because everything seemed so big, and in our trepidation we clung to Granny who had taken Mum's place in our affections. How it must have upset Mum and Dad, and spoiled our reunion, suspecting we had forgotten them, which we had. Granny and Grandad stayed on for a few days until we had all settled down and got to know one another again. Then they returned home, Grandad no doubt with relief, and Granny to a nest empty of "Her Little Chicks". We were never to live in Horsforth again, but we visited often. Mum referred to it as home and always spoke of it as such, remembering the "old days" with Dad pretty often.

Our first days in Bolton were uneventful, and we weren't allowed out to play on our own like we were in Blackpool, because of the traffic on the main road. Not that there was much in those days, but the buses trundled past at regular intervals, their wheels making a loud noise on the cobbled road which still contained the tram lines of a past era. We played around the house and bakehouse. Mum did her best to keep us out of the shop, but she wasn't always successful and she must have had her hands full at times, shooing us out to "Go and pester Dad". One of her most uttered sayings when we were growing up was "I wish my name was Dad", used often and stoically when under siege for a lolly or sweets at dinnertime and after school when we hung around bored. Dad's helper, Agnes, somewhat older than Mum and Dad, became a stand-in Granny. When Mum was busy in the shop, she took us under her wing without a murmur, setting us to play with bits of dough and pastry, a good substitute for plasticine, and a rolling pin. We made dollies and "gingerbread men" and little mice, the pastry becoming dirtier in the process. Afterwards we gave them to Dad to bake in the big oven, poring over them excitedly to see them as they came out baked, dirt and all. They were never fit to eat after all the handling and scraping up from the floor where they had been dropped a time or two, and when our attention was taken by something else, they were relegated to the pig swill bag and forgotten.

Mum put our names down at Sunninghill School at the top end of Derby Street, about a mile away — we were to start when we turned five.

CHAPTER
THREE

Play Days and
School Days

In our early days in Bolton, we never needed to be woken by Mum. Dad rose early. His day started prompt at four a.m., when he would creep downstairs and draw the curtains back. After making his morning cuppa, he began his baking, starting with mixing the bread dough, which he then left to rise before he "knocked it back" and weighed it into loaf-sized pieces on an old pair of bakehouse scales, ready to be kneaded and shaped to fit into the loaf tins. Once filled, they were put into the proving cabinet to rise and fill the tins in the steamy heat provided by a pan of boiling water on the very bottom of the cabinet, which he was careful never to let boil dry.

We could usually gauge the time by the noises coming up the stairs and through the window. A clatter of clogs, rising to a crescendo, warned us that the day was about to start for the mill workers, who turned the corner into Mather Street to enter through the mill gates, and when the hooter went they sharpened into a quicker step as the late comers hurried into work, and finally died away altogether as the gates closed and the machinery started up. This was Dad's signal to bring Mum a cup of tea as her day was about to start also, and she set about the task of parting us from our beds and overseeing the washing of our hands and faces, making sure our necks were clean, something we always managed to overlook if not supervised. The shop opened at nine o'clock when, with us hopefully "sorted", she would start to fill the window with cakes and still warm loaves in two sizes, large tin and small tin, baked now with a delicious crispy crust, shiny and brown on top.

A variety of freshly baked egg custards, tea cakes, sweet and sticky on top, and Dad's famous oven-bottomed flour cakes would be brought through in large rough wooden trays, hot from the oven, filling the house and shop with the aroma of freshly baked bread. Dad would "cop it" from Mum for not wiping his feet on the doormat and leaving a trail of floury footprints across the coconut matting in the living room which he had to cross to get into the shop. Delicious pies and pasties soon followed, to be displayed with the "morning goods" in time for the mill workers' mid-morning break, when they would tumble through the shop door, jostling to be first in the queue. Woe betide anyone with a list. Mum would have to shout for Dad and Agnes to help serve in the frantic ten minutes or so before they dashed back to work, some with empty hands. Thwarted and cursing at the sound of the hooter which had robbed them of their pie, their hunger pangs having to wait to be banished until dinnertime, and glancing enviously at the luckier ones who had been served.

Housewives on their morning sally to the shops would follow, often lingering to chat. Mum would carry on serving while all topics were discussed, from who had died to the latest goings on at the house of ill repute just across the road, a great source of interest in the neighbourhood, and of which we had a good view of the carryings on. Shopping in those days necessitated a visit to the grocer's, greengrocer's, butcher's and the local hardware store, as supermarkets were still a thing of the future. People shopped daily; refrigerators were not a part of the kitchen as they are today, so any perishables had to bought on the day. Milk was delivered daily by the milkman on his rounds, just enough to last the day; any more meant waste as it just wouldn't keep. Bread was baked and shopped for every day, none of the wrapped variety so common today which will keep up to a week if not opened. The older customers would often check for freshness with a sly squeeze, frowned on by Mum if she saw them and a "Don't touch, we don't know where you've 'ad yer 'ands".

Clogs and shawls were a common sight. Where we lived all the old women wore them, mostly in black signifying widowhood, or maybe they didn't require washing quite so often in that colour; whichever it was, it made them look older than their years. The taking of snuff, a dirty habit according to Mum, made the end of their noses and fingers brown, and we shied away from them in disgust and fear in case they were witches. They certainly looked like them to us.

The dinnertime rush began at twelve when the hooter would go and the scramble began all over again, with Mum, Dad and Agnes serving. The till rang out, dinging continuously as they all pressed down on the pound, shilling and pence levers to ring up the prices, the queue seemingly getting longer as more mill-workers fought to get served with Dad's popular meat and potato pies that would fill any hunger pangs until teatime. Once the big rush had gone, along with all the pies, we had our own dinner, with Mum jumping up at intervals at the sound of the shop bell to serve any late comers. Often her dinner was had in stages, after many a "put my dinner in the oven" was shouted through to the living room where the drop-leaf table had us gathered around, which meant dashing with the plate to the oven in the kitchen in the effort to keep it warm till she could get to eat it. The afternoon was often "slack" so Dad managed to have a nap.

Most of the shopping was done in the morning, and, after the washing up was done and Dad had woken up, Mum often managed to "nip out", leaving Dad in charge while she did so. She then shopped for us at the neighbourhood shops, or would nip down to the market on market days. Sometimes she took us with her, but mostly she went on her own. It was the cheapest place to shop for anything but not always the wisest, and she would dash off on her own so she could have a good look before she bought anything. When she came back, Dad would clean up the mess in the bakehouse. That included scrubbing down the two big wooden tables, sweeping up the trodden-in flour and pastry from the floor, and swilling out with a stiff bristle brush and lots of water the residue of the flour that remained.

We would help, often more of a hindrance than help, and we would all play "Pooh sticks" in the milky stream that flowed down the gutter and into the grate at the end of the back street, cheering on our spent match stalk in its race down to the grate, often cheating as it became wedged on some gunge, poking it off with a stick to speed it on its way. Mum would close the shop at six, often leaving the door unlocked to let in anyone "cheeky" who rang the bell to pick up something they had forgotten. After that we sat at the table to have our tea of Dad's fresh bread and butter and potted meat and a cake, the usual limited choice of what there was left. In the summer we played out in the back street till bedtime. In winter we huddled in front of the fire, developing our "Corned beef legs", the unsightly result of too much heat on bare legs, which Mum would rue in the summer when she cast off her stockings, scrubbing at her shins to reduce the blotchy mess caused by their toasting in front of the fire.

Sometimes we played card games, Happy Families, Old Maid or a rousing game of Snap, around the table until it was time for bed, which always came around too quickly. Then, after we were in bed, Mum and Dad listened to the wireless, finally putting out the stairs light when we had gone to sleep and having a bit of peace and quiet before they went to bed themselves. The wireless was our best form of entertainment in the evenings, and we were all fans of Al Read, *Life with the Lyons, Take It from Here*, Archie Andrews, and *The Glums*. On Sundays a special treat was *Journey into Space*, in which we followed Lemmy and his companions on a scary trip to Mars.

When Mum decided it was time for bed we had to go, no argument. Up the stairs we were hustled, begging for a bit longer to no avail, to have our faces, necks and knees scrubbed and flannelled and rubbed briskly dry on a rough towel, tucked into bed and kissed goodnight. Because we were afraid of the dark, the stairs light was left on for a while and Dad would be greeted by a wail of protest if he turned it off before we had gone to sleep. Then we would hear Mum telling him off for turning it off too soon, and be wide awake again.

Such was the ebb and flow of our younger days, when we would play, and squabble in the yard or the back street, closed to traffic and ending in a cul-de-sac with a piece of waste land where two houses had been demolished. It was a dirty place to play. The ash and cinders from the mill furnaces were tipped into a square pit on the mill side of the street at the top of the cul-de-sac. It drew us like a magnet, climbing up the huge pile of cinders to run down them crunching as we went. Mum must have despaired at the state of our white cotton socks as she gathered us up for bed, scrubbing at the cindery knees.

She began to talk of "when we go to school", as the time drew near, and eventually the day dawned when we were hustled there, shining, subdued and full of

45

trepidation. We entered the school yard to be met with a wall of noise, and were taken up an enormous wide stone staircase to see Miss Wood, who looked like Jane Wyman, Mum said, with the face of a nun. She took us across the hall and down two flights of stone steps into the basement nursery class. The room was full of other children, toys, small chairs and, dominating it, a large sandpit, complete with buckets and spades. Remembering Blackpool, we made a beeline for the sandpit, and next time we looked for Mum, she was nowhere to be seen. With us engrossed in our sand pies, she had taken the opportunity to slip away unnoticed, hoping the sandpit would fill our interest until she came to collect us. It was not to be. Feeling deserted, we headed for the door unnoticed, and actually made it into the school yard just in time to see her going out of the gate.

You could say all hell broke loose as we were sussed, and taken back in a state of distress and floods of tears to the nursery class by Miss Wood, on patrol in the school yard for escapers. Once pacified by the promise of Mum coming back for us at dinnertime, we began to play, and in no time at all she was back to pick us up. Admittedly we weren't too keen to go the next day, but once left we were kept well-occupied, to prevent any re-occurrence of the events of the previous day. Broken into school, we soon settled down and acquired shoe bags and coat pegs with our names on in the little cloakroom in the nursery. Admittedly, they found it difficult to tell which of us was which, and we soon got into the habit of answering to either name, presenting them with two little girls, instead of one.

In all we spent five happy years there. The first two years were spent in the nursery class and Miss Flynn's, also in the basement. Mum blamed our constant coughs and colds on that, although in my later experience as a mother, between five and seven are the years children are most susceptible to the germs and viruses of their world. We certainly were, going through measles, mumps and chickenpox in quick succession. Jean, always the most vulnerable of the two of us, got scarlet fever as well, which Mum blamed on the paddling pool in Queens Park. I had to sleep in Mum and Dad's room, away from her, while she was quarantined in our bedroom, with an airwick pull-up stick, and a wet blanket hung over the door frame to stop the germs getting out. Mum wouldn't let me near her, and we had to shout to one another through the door, with me sitting at the top of the stairs missing her dreadfully.

Mum spoiled her atrociously with Peter Rabbit books and she would taunt me with them through the wet blanket. I was envious of the Peter Rabbit books. Mum wouldn't let me read them because of the germs, and I was pretty upset when they were burnt on the fire when Jean was better, as everything was to stop the infection spreading. In those day it was a notifiable disease, and when Mum had had it as a child she was taken to the fever hospital, and left with a hearing loss, due to the nerve damage it caused. Nevertheless, those Peter Rabbit books were a bone of contention between us for quite a while; the very mention of them would

47

cause a scrap, and to this day Peter Rabbit holds a fatal fascination for me.

To give her credit, Mum always came up trumps when we were ill. A fire was lit in the bedroom fireplace and stoked regularly, to "sweat it out of us". She spoiled us rotten with colouring books and crayons, and made us her homemade lemonade with fresh lemons and lots of honey, to soothe our sore throats. We were given hot mustard baths that would now verge on child cruelty, one of Dad's sworn-by remedies, and put to roast in front of a roaring fire. Sometimes the cure was worse than the disease, but as children do we soon bounced back, with abundant energy, and returned to school with a note to keep the truant officer at bay. Sometimes we were given that old fashioned "cure all", syrup of figs, and dispatched to school with a note to warn the teacher of our frequent and impending departures to the toilet block at the bottom of the yard. At the onset of a warning twinge a hand would be raised in the hope of quickly being given consent to leave the room, to the knowing sniggering of other pupils who had also at some time or another suffered the same dire fate. And we would hurry pink faced to our ablutions, with the hope that we made it in time, and a pair of spare knickers in our pocket. Both Mum and Granny's generation were obsessed with their bowels, an occupation that has thankfully faded with their demise.

At times we brought home from school unwanted guests, caught from other children. Head lice were a scourge. Although inspected regularly by the nit nurse we called Nitty Nora, we were occasionally sent home with a note, handed out to the culprits at the end of the inspection. It was always shameful to receive one, and even more so to have to give it to Mum who then knew you had been playing with the "dirty children" she had told you not to play with. After administering a scolding, Mum would get out the Derbac soap and the fine tooth comb, and the nit picking sessions would ensue. First the foul smelling stuff would be lathered up on our heads and left to do its worst, and we were then made to stand for what seemed like hours while she combed the nits and lice out of our heads. This shaming performance would go on daily till we were clear, when she would dispatch us to school with a "don't play with the dirty kids, or we'll have 'em again". Of course we did; there was no distinction to us, they were all our playmates. Some of the children in our class had no Mums and it showed. When we sat on the school pipes to warm our bums, the stench of wet knickers picked out the unfortunate ones. Sadly it was not their fault, and most of the Dads did their best, but there were one or two who had to be taken in hand by the teachers, and a note sent to their Dads.

Dirt wasn't an issue in our house. We were plonked in the bath regularly, one at either end. The issue of who had to sit at the plug end was hotly disputed, with the one who lost emerging pink and shining and a dimple where the plug had been. Hair washing wasn't too pleasant either, with the water too hot or too cold, jugged over our heads in the bath, with shampoo running down our faces and into our eyes in the process. Any squeals were met with "pride's painful", and there was never any sympathy dished out to smarting eyes, the job being done as quickly as possible in the unheated bathroom. At times Mum was a frustrated hairdresser, perming our hair at regular intervals with a home perm, a process that was agony. It took hours while she pulled and scraped every scrap of hair into tight little curlers, doused it with burning perming lotion, and then covered our heads with froth, which ran down into our smarting eyes as we grumbled about the time it took. The final indignity was when she tried to flatten it to our heads with Amami setting lotion, a slimy concoction with a funny smell. Many a cuff had ensured we sat perfectly still during the process, while she pushed and preened it into shape. We hated it, and dreaded going to school the next day to be sniggered at. Our heads would be sore for a week, and finally after many years of suffering we rebelled, but that was years later, well into our teens.

After two years in the juniors, we moved upstairs to Mrs. Brown's class, leaving the lovely Miss Flynn behind in the basement. Mrs. Brown taught us to read from little cards, which told a simple story, and started us on writing, printing the letters. It was simple and easy to learn. We also did sums, simple addition and subtraction. The difficult bits were to come later. Mrs. Brown was not one of our favourite teachers, like the gentle Miss Flynn. She shouted! We learned discipline, and had to sit where we were put, not with each other, as she couldn't tell us apart. We had country dancing lessons too because Mrs. Brown played the piano; we went dancing round the school hall without much grace, and with Geoffrey, who always had a candle from his nose. She played the piano in assembly too, her lack of musical finesse sending titters among the juniors who, having by now learned the school hymns, picked out her wrong notes and pauses while attempting to regain her place after she had played off-key.

At Christmas, we had school parties, making paper chains from sticky paper for Mrs. Brown to hang up across the ceiling and from wall to wall. For the party on the last day of school, we brought jelly and sandwiches and fairy cakes, all home-made. Simple and cheap, but often by the time we had got them to the classroom they were a bit squashed, and the jelly, wobbly to start with, had a tendency to slip all over the plate. We all made our own paper hats out of crêpe paper and gum, which was painted on out of a jam jar with a big paintbrush that Mrs. Brown kept tight control of, in case it was splashed about by the exuberant, excited small boys whose every attempt to snatch off our paper hats at the party were usually successful, causing tears as we surveyed the torn bits of coloured paper we had worked so hard on. We played Musical Chairs with great gusto, with lots of bumping and pushing involved, giving us an excuse for a quick bash back in retribution for a torn hat, while Mrs. Brown sat with her back to us at the piano. Once the tea was had and the jelly eaten and the Musical Chairs over, we were "surprised" by a visit from Santa, who delved deep into his sack and found a gift for each of us. Much fun was had in the exchanging of our presents before we went home, and we usually managed to find something suitable each, despite the odd bit of falling out. By the time all the Mums turned up to clear up the mess and claim all the labelled cutlery and empty jelly, cake and tea plates, we were all tuckered out, and they would gather us up and take us home, excitement over for another year, thank goodness.

Mum made us stay to school dinners after a while, but we only lasted a week, it was so horrible. The meals were delivered in big aluminium drums, and always consisted of lumpy mash, stewed meat of unknown origin, with some kind of vegetable, often cabbage, and a stodgy dumpling to fill us up cheaply. Puddings weren't much better either, suet or sponge, heavy and sticky, served with a thick lumpy custard, not very hot. We had to take the money for them on a Monday morning, along with our saving stamp money, being called up one by one to hand the money to the teacher, who marked it down in her book. Some of the children whose parents were poor got their dinners free. We always knew who they were, because they never got up to take money to the teacher when we did, but were always there lined up with us to go into the dinner room. I suppose today it would be a bit of a stigma, but then no one bothered at all. It was like that, lots of them got them for free, there was never any taunting about it.

Poverty wasn't all that shameful, no-one kept up with the Joneses, we just all helped each other, and Mums passed on the clothes we had grown out of to other

Mums who found it harder to manage. I know our Mum did; she passed our grown-out-of things on to other women who had large families, some of them living in the terraced streets around us. Shaw Street and Pilkington Street were two such examples. Built in the Victorian era, the narrow houses all had cellars and attics. They were entered up a flight of stone steps to the front door, which in my childhood always seemed to be open. Sometimes a different family lived in the lower part, closed off from the posher top part, which had donkey-stoned steps, the donkey-stone being obtained from the rag and bone man in exchange for a few cast-off clothes that had seen better days.

The rag and bone man was a common sight then, with his barrow, and his shout of "rag bone" as he trailed the streets, and his donkey-stone was a popular item because most housewives did their steps at least once a week, a source of great pride despite the poorness of the area. A rickety rail accompanied the steps, and in summer the families would sit out and chat, a tier of neighbours, exchanging the local gossip, preferable to sitting in the small kitchen-come-living room where they made their meals on the coal fired ranges, and kept the ever-boiling kettle ready for the constant "cuppas" they held in their hands. Most of these houses had parlours where visitors were seated. Unused most of the time, except for special occasions like Christmas and Easter, they were closed up to every day use, and kept for "best". Woe betide any kids who ran amok there among the treasures kept from everyday use.

There were many streets like this in Bolton when I was a child, before the general slum clearance of the 1950s. Unlike today, when you can walk down a street and not see a soul, these streets were teeming with kids and women in clogs and shawls, standing chatting. They were generally sociable places, with the kids of the street playing street games, and we joined in many a game of Hopscotch and Tig. The families, though many of them were what Mum called rough and ready, were good to us, sharing what little they had, even though we were often sent home to beg a cake or two on their kids' behalf. It was a happy place to play, despite the poverty all around us, which at the time we never noticed.

Carey Street, at the back of Crook Street, now long gone, was a different story. A ride along there on our bikes was positively dangerous, and foolish. A cobblestone street from the 1800s, the houses were in a sad state of repair, and probably bug and vermin ridden, every family having nothing but umpteen kids. To venture there to ride through the puddles on our bikes usually meant a stone in our direction, and a mouth full of abuse. We used to dare one another to ride down Carey Street. Usually it was a ride into Hell, and we would pedal back scared out of our wits, dodging the missiles, hearts pounding, as we rode up the back street into the safety of our cul-de-sac.

One place we used to go to play regularly was the convent, belonging to St. Peter and St. Paul's. Various children were fostered by the nuns there, and one by the name of May, who was about sixteen, worked for

Dad. She was lovely and we would go back with her to play with the other children. Mum didn't really like us going there, because there was also a soup kitchen which attracted tramps from far and near. Admittedly they were there for the soup, but they were somewhat smelly, hanging about and dossing on the pavement. One night, long after the soup kitchen had closed, we had a tramp come into the shop who wouldn't go. Finding the soup kitchen closed, he staged a sit-in on the floor of the shop. He was in a dreadful state, but Dad, feeling sorry for him, made him a drink on the condition that he would leave after he had drunk it, causing Mum to lock the shop door in the future to keep any others out. She had wanted to call a policeman but Dad wouldn't let her, the poor soul was starving. He hung about for a few days, then disappeared. There were loads of tramps about in those days. Dad always said they were ex-soldiers who had served in the war and couldn't settle down again, and was sympathetic really, being an ex-soldier himself.

In Bolton, after the war, there were lots of churches and chapels of all denominations. In our neighbourhood we had a Roman Catholic church, a Methodist chapel, a Church of England, a Congregational church, and various other religious organisations, including the Salvation Army, who had local premises in the town. All had a good social programme of events, and were well-attended at the time. We went to Fletcher Street Methodist Church, keeping up the tradition of the Brownies (Mum had been a Brown Owl in her youth before she met Dad). It consisted of a nice if somewhat small church, and a separate Sunday School, very musty with that distinctive "chapel smell" that pervades all old churches despite their upkeep. The area around was pebbled in seaside pebbles, with flat grave slabs from the early 1800s spaced closely about. At the time we were very disrespectful, because we used to jump from one to another while we waited for the caretaker to let us in. He always used to threaten to tell Mum if he caught us, chasing us if we were cheeky to him, but he couldn't run far because his legs were bandy through rickets. He and his wife were very devoted to the chapel and kept it immaculate and shining despite its age. In later years it became an Indian supermarket, and the grave stones had cars parked on them, which I suppose didn't matter any more, because all the people who cared about the poor buried people would be dead themselve anyway, including poor Mr. and Mrs. Entwistle who devoted so much time to the place.

We attended Sunday School there as well, and sang in the choir occasionally, not that we wanted to but we were rounded up to "do our bit" as Mum called it when we were dispatched to church as part of the Brownie pack, shining with soap, gleaming with brass badges, and smelling of Brasso. After Sunday dinner we were sent right back to attend the Sunday School session while Mum and Dad had their nap. Again we would sing hymns and pray for "little children", which included us, and then split up into groups according to our age to have Bible stories, which seemed interminable and through which we would fidget with our little books, waiting for the golden star, a record of our attendance, to be stamped in them. Then it was the sermon and prayers again before being sent back into the world, all the better for the experience, to unleash our energy on Mum and Dad. Despite all our attendances, we only once got a book at Christmas, as those who were in the top attendance group did, and in time we would sneak out and back home to play in the back street until we could show our faces at home when Sunday School was supposed to have finished.

The Brownies were a very different kettle of fish. We played games and went on outings to the park and the Jumbles, a pretty woodland valley with a river running through it. Later it was flooded to make a reservoir, but when we knew it, it was a little paradise. As Brownies, we would occasionally go on Saturdays in summer, taking our jam butties and Spanish pop, which was a bottle of water with black ha'penny Spanish in the bottom shaken until it was dissolved, for a picnic. We could have taken better sandwiches, but it all added to the occasion and Spanish pop didn't explode if it was shaken up as we ran about. Brown Owl would tell us about the types of trees, and wild flowers and birds, then taking off our shoes and socks we would all wade in the stream looking at the minnows and tadpoles, if there were any. It was very educational, besides being a fun day out, and it was always a tired little pack of Brownies that climbed back up the path to catch the bus home and tell our Mums all about it.

The pack meetings through the week were fun too. Shining a penny up with brass polish for hours (the old smooth ones being the best), to take to lay in a long line

57

on the floor, and then to sing and dance around it. Then we would take our "Badges" for things like setting a table or parting our hair, going to Brown Owl's house where, on completion of the task, she gave us a cloth badge to sew onto our Brownie dress, inspecting the sewing at the next meeting. Of course we used to cheat because Mum always sewed them on, and we received full marks for sewing. It was all good fun in a rather naïve way, a "camp silliness" I suppose, but at the time it was great fun, and taught us a few things we wouldn't have learned if left to our own devices.

The summer evenings spent in the park were good fun too, especially if the Cubs, who had the next room to us, went as well. Then it would be a case of competition as to who won the most games and tasks we were set, often breaking into fisticuffs between us all, when the Cubs called us names and threw grass at us in the proceedings, especially if they were losing. It all faded into insignificance, however, when Tawny Owl's little girl joined the pack and was made leader of the "Elves". Jean refused to go again, saying it was favouritism, so that was that. Eventually the Sunday School faded away too, because Tawny Owl was one of the leading lights there too. It was all very sad. We missed the potato pie suppers, and all the dances where we did the Paul Jones and the Hoky Coky, but Dad still did the plaited sheaf of corn for the Harvest Festival and supper, taking us with him to set it up on the church altar. We always went to the evening supper with Mum and Dad, because Dad always made the potato pie in two big bowls in his oven for them, and we all went to dish it onto plates from a long table at the end of the room. It was very enjoyable with dancing and a lot of jollity in the school hall, where we all sat on the school benches around the room.

Another of our favourite pastimes was a visit to the sweet shop, despite sugar rationing being in force for quite a while after the war. This was Mum's excuse to keep our consumption of sweets pretty low but even so we still managed to spend the ration every week, running down to Mr. Costello's with our threepenny bit and the ration book tight in our hands, staring in the window at the array of jars and tins of toffee displayed on the shelves. Sweets like penny chews and blackjacks came ready wrapped, but most had to be weighed out on Mr. Costello's scales, scrutinised carefully to make sure he didn't take one off he should have left on, which he was known to do if not watched carefully. Mr. Costello's shop was an old-fashioned sweet shop, with counters in an L shape. One was highly polished and held the all-important brass scales, and a round rubber mat, on which you put your money. The other had a hinged flap, which could be raised to give access to either side of the counter through a small door, and also led directly into the back living room, closed off by a heavy curtain. He was an old man. Mum used to say he was eighty, and he had an invalid wife who we never saw but frequently heard, shouting through to him in a loud voice, "Billy, 'ave yer a minute", making all and sundry jump in the shop. Though none as much as Mr.

59

Costello, who nipped smartly through the curtain at her command. He was small, with white hair thinning on top, was very pasty, and stooped, no doubt through the hours spent ducking through the curtain between the customers and his ailing wife, and he had a dewdrop at the end of his nose which occasionally dripped off. Dad always used to joke about it when we offered him a sweet, and pretend his sweet was wet, laughing as we peered closely at it. It was always the hope that we got the sweets before the dewdrop dripped, dreading to see that it had gone when he handed us the sweets, and not actually knowing where it had dripped, hopefully not in our cornet bag as he folded it carefully to tuck in the corners.

A lot of our time was spent in Mr. Costello's, and all our pocket money, buying Rainbow Crystals, flavoured coloured sugar to dip our wet forefinger in, Roocrofts Tics, little liquorice cushions that lasted ages and left our mouths black, Coltsfoot rock, red hot and sucked to a smooth point, and liquorice sticks, chewed to a stringy mess by which time all the flavour had gone. Gobstoppers really were enormous, their coloured layers examined every few minutes by sticky fingers as we pulled them out of our mouths to see what colour came next. Mum would give us the ration book, with a "see he doesn't take more than he should", and a threepenny bit each, and off we would race down to the shop, often taking a half hour or so to make up our minds on what to spend the precious money and coupon. Granted he was very patient with us but he was always hovering between the counter and the curtained doorway, ready to dive either way on demand.

Mr. Costello's was also a temperance bar, and he sold hot Vimto, and sarsaparilla in thick glass tumblers, which his customers drank while sitting on the old school bench he provided down one side of his shop. The Vimto was a bit weak, not like the one sold in Tognarelli's in town, which was thick and sticky. When we were older, we would go to Manfredi's near High Street and the swimming baths; there was nothing like hot Vimto to warm you and set your teeth on edge after an hour in High Street swimming baths had left you with goose pimples. Thinking back, we consumed quite a bit of the old sweet stuff despite the rationing, and Dad would pull our legs when our teeth started to fall out, leaving us with gaps at the front. They would start to go wobbly, giving us something to play with for hours, wobbling them this way and that. Mum said when she was a girl it was the done thing to tie them to the door knob with a bit of string, then stand with your back to the door while someone slammed it sharply, pulling out the tooth. We were not convinced, preferring the horribly wobbly tooth, and eventually wobbling it loose enough to fall out, with a squeal of relief, and the promise of a visit from the tooth fairy in the offing if we put it under the rug in front of the fire. Next day it was the first thing we did, check the rug in hope of finding a sixpence in place of the tooth, which was duly handed to Mr. Costello as quick as we could get there.

Needless to say a visit to the school clinic and the dentist was called for in later years when the double milk teeth started to decay, a far worse experience than a visit from the tooth fairy. What's more, they often kept the tooth because we were too groggy to ask for it on coming around from the gas, and Mum would console us with the sixpence anyway for what we had endured at the school clinic in Flash Street.

CHAPTER
FOUR

Neighbours

Living on a main road meant most of our neighbours were shopkeepers and publicans. We even had a brothel nearby, closely watched by everybody and a great source of amusement. It did quite a brisk trade. On our block were a furniture shop, a wallpaper shop, a gents' outfitters, us, a tripe shop, a greengrocer's, and a catering hardware shop. Across the road we had the Progress Stores which sold everything, a rooming house (containing the brothel), a grocer's, a barbershop, and a second wallpaper shop in a big double fronted house with a forecourt which must have been quite impressive in its better days. That was our close environment, along with the mill across the back street. There were four public houses within a hundred yards. They were the Grey Man, the Peacock, the Good Samaritan, and the Derby Arms, all doing a good trade, or so it appeared from the daily deliveries Dad made. On the corner of the next block up was Dr. Ryan's, where they made surgical appliances and the famous Dr. Ryan's pills, a cure-all for every known disease. Mum always called them Dr. Ryan's pea green pills, so she must have tried them. Dad reserved his comments to "quack

quack" and waddling like a duck at the mention of them. Further up that block was a butcher's, another small baker's who specialised in making crumpets and potato cakes which they sold wholesale, a chemist's, the Good Samaritan, several terraced houses and another grocer's shop. Down the road, on the next block adjacent, were various shops selling second-hand clothing, sweets (Mr. Costello's), newspapers, second-hand furniture and household goods, and a café where they let you take away meals providing you promised to bring back the plate, with a small deposit ensuring you did. Several old people took their own plate, thus saving on the deposit and journey back with the plate. It was quite common to see them passing the shop, with plate and a clean tea-towel to keep in the heat tucked under their arm. There was also a ladies' hairdressers on the block where all the local gossip changed hands, and no doubt was added to in the process, especially the latest goings on at the brothel of which we all had a good view.

Across the road from that block, the road split into two. Moor Lane curved down towards the market and Derby Street became Great Moor Street, carrying straight on to cross Newport Street, the main shopping street of Bolton, which led to the town hall square and the bigger town shops of the town. Between Great Moor Street and Moor Lane was Derby Street School, a big Victorian building in red brick with two separate entrances segregating boys and girls, although it was later turned over to girls only, but we never went there. When we first lived there the road had blue stone sets with tram lines in, and a horse trough at the junction where the road split. The horse trough was there for years, and I remember it well into the late 1950s. The road was tarmacked earlier than that, and when we were very young the trolley buses were the main form of transport up and down Derby Street, replacing the trams of the previous period.

The furniture shop at the end or our block was Tower's, run by a quiet-spoken Scotsman by the name of Jock, and a fly-by-night with a Clark Gable moustache called Harry. They were always popping in and out for pies, and used to chat to Dad a lot over the back door while they were loading furniture into their van in the back street. All smoked cigarettes, passing them around as they swapped army experiences and gossip, while they had a "minute for a docker", as Dad called these chats in the back street. Sometimes the main topic of discussion was the latest bone of contention with Billy Pike, whose access to his garage was often blocked by delivery vans either to our bakehouse or Tower's shop back entrance, at the top of the cul-de-sac.

Belle, who had the wallpaper shop, was very close with them, and she used to pop in for a chat with Mum when she was "slack" in the afternoons. Mum was always popping in there too, often borrowing the big wallpaper pattern books to look at. We were always decorating, or seemed to be, with the dampness of the place, and we knew it was in the offing when the wallpaper books appeared. Given a scraper each, we would set to work on the walls, peeling at the bottom from the condensation. Eventually Dad got fed up, and wood-panelled the bottom half in hardboard to hide the peeling and the mould. Once he attempted to paper the ceiling to cover the cracks, but the paper wouldn't stick and became wrapped around his head and shoulders, giving us a lot of amusement, until he lost his sense of humour and swapped what was left of it for distemper instead. The wallpapers were always a bit garish by today's standards, in squares or lines with dots or squiggles on grey, beige or white backgrounds. Red and grey were the fashionable colours and we had it everywhere, except in the kitchen where it clashed with Mum's yellow kitchenette. That was always painted cream for as long as I can remember, in a gloss paint so she could wash it when it got yellow from the gas stove, and cooking.

We got rid of Dad's old leather armchair when the stuffing popped out, and bought a red cut-moquette cottage suite with wooden arms from Jock and Harry, who carried it down the back street, and through the bakehouse to be admired in the living room by the four of us, not daring to sit on it in case we spoiled it. We still kept the coconut matting though; it just wouldn't wear out. Every so often we would roll it up and clean underneath, laughing at the pattern the flour had made through the gaps. Lasted for years, did that coconut matting, until eventually Mum, getting sick at the sight of it, put in a carpet square instead. We were glad to see it go too; it played havoc with our knees and the toes of our shoes when we played on the floor. Once we got a carpet, we thought we were posh, and we had to take off our shoes to walk on it, Dad as well. Then the novelty of it wore off and it was treated like the coconut matting, but the bits of pastry that got stuck to it from Dad's feet didn't come off half so well.

Next door to us lived Dad's arch enemy, Billy Pike. Generally known as "Pike's High Class Gents Outfitters", Billy, his wife Elsie, son John, and Monty, the most imperious of cats who often appeared on our coke hole roof to partake of the heat rising from Dad's oven stokehole, were all well-attired and well-shod. Though the shop was small, it was well-fitted out, as most outfitters of that era were, exuding an air of good living and upper class wealth, somewhat out of place in Derby Street and in a small shop. The walls contained shelves and drawers in mahogany, well-polished, and all labelled and sized. A hat stand displayed cloth caps, jaunty and plain, trilbys, and homburgs in all colours and tweeds, and the shop sold good quality shirts, slacks and blazers, sports jackets and shooting jackets, ties, cravats and socks. Suits were made to measure, which explained the tape measure always hanging around Billy's neck. He was haughty and thin, with a hawk-like beak, thin lips and piercing eyes; his wife Elsie was the opposite, plump and jolly with a roll of grey hair pinned in a sausage around her neck, around which also hung a tape measure. She was a Londoner and talked a bit posh when she came into the shop to buy her bread.

Despite their hatred of one another, Dad wore Pike's apparel and Billy ate Dad's pies. At Christmas they would bring their turkey around for Dad to cook in the big oven, along with several others the neighbours had brought for him to cook. I don't know why, but it was always Billy Pike's turkey the cat "got at". More than once Dad had to explain the mutilation away, with the cat hovering on the periphery. One Christmas we even swapped it for ours when it was discovered missing a leg and the parson's nose, and displaying a mutilated left breast, Mum doctoring it up for us while Dad brayed the cat in a futile attempt to teach it a lesson once and for all. They kept a civilised feud going for years, despite the efforts of both parties to live in harmony. Jealousy of each other's cars played a good part in the animosity, each having to outdo the other, Mr. Pike running a succession of smart Vanguards, and Dad a string of old bangers. Eventually Dad put Billy's nose out of joint when he bought a newish Sunbeam Talbot in "metallic blue". They would discuss the merits of every car they bought in the back street, seemingly good friends, only to fall out the following week when Dad's car was blocking the entrance to Billy's garage once more. Mr. Pike, immaculately clad, and Dad in his whites and mucky pinny, arms up to the elbows white with flour, would go at it hammer and tongs until one of them banged in, purple with rage. A state of silence then existed between them for a while, until one or the other ventured a friendly word to test the temperature of the water, but they still bought the bread and pies despite all the rows.

One of their biggest shouting matches occurred in the summer months, when Mr. Pike would display his "high class apparel" outside the shop to catch the eye of the "hoi polloi" passing trade. Our shop front, no expense spared, had acquired a sun canopy to keep the afternoon sun off Dad's fancy cakes. It was a stretch of white canvas sheeting on a frame, which was pulled manually with the aid of a long hooked pole from its casing above the window and down to shade the shop front. Dad had found it stiff to pull out, and had used his cure-all, bakehouse lard, to grease the vertical poles on which the dratted mechanism slid. Billy, being Billy, had used the poles on which to display his blazers, despite them being on our property. All hell was let loose on the discovery that Dad's bakehouse lard, by now a runny slick of grease, had pooled on his best blazers. Blood up, he made a beeline for Dad and dragged him outside to inspect the blazers. Dad, who never hesitated to look for a gas leak with a lighted match and was generally prone to living dangerously, told him in no uncertain terms where to go and sling his hook and the dratted blazers, and a shouting match ensued. Only the intervention of Mum and Mrs. Pike prevented punches being thrown and the bobby being sent for. To give Dad his due, that day he wiped the floor with Mr. Pike, and there was a long silence between them for quite a while eventually the incident faded into memory and relations resumed as normal in an uneasy peace. Their son John was ten years older than us and prone to having fits. He was kept close at hand and had to help in the shop. He was rather a dandy, with the ever-present tape measure around his neck, and we would tease him unmercifully, climbing onto their sloping garage roof and shouting to him to find our ball when we hadn't lost it. When we really had lost it over in their back yard, we would creep into their shop and politely ask for it back, with Mr. Pike sending poor John into the back yard to find it and throw it back over the wall. Sometimes we were sent off with a flea in our ear when they were all too busy to look for it or were not speaking to Dad, and made us wait until it was discovered and thrown back. Either way we must have been a nuisance to them, I suppose.

On the other side was a tripe shop run by an old lady, Mrs. Jones, and her spinster daughter, "our Annie". Their window was full of white wobbly tripe, black puddings and brawn, a sort of jellied potted meat made from pigs' heads. Pigs' feet were displayed on a marble slab in the window bottom, and always held a fatal fascination for us, poor things. It all looked and smelled disgusting. Occasionally Mum would send us errands for some black pudding for Dad's tea. It was made from pigs' blood, and if you poked out the bits of white fat it was quite tasty but somewhat peppery; Dad had it boiled, with bread and butter and a dash of mustard. Mum would poke out the fat because it was gristly, but we weren't too keen on it, knowing where it had come from. Mrs. Jones was old like our Granny and wore the same cross-over pinny. Annie was courting Arnold who worked in the mill at the back. He was a lot older than her and Mum said he was married, so it was all probably in vain. We didn't take much notice; they weren't very interesting anyway, and disappeared in the end. We certainly didn't miss the tripe, that's for sure.

Next door to the tripe shop were the Farrs, our best friends on the block. Mr. and Mrs. Farr were the same age as Mum and Dad, and their son Graham was a year older than we were. They moved in a couple of years after us, and had the greengrocer's. Mrs. Farr, Lily to Mum, ran the shop, while Joe worked at Hick Hargreave's, engineers in Crook Street, as a labourer. Graham was our best friend, and we all played together in the back street. When it rained, as it did often, we played in one of our houses, with Graham's matchbox cars, dashing between houses when the Mums got fed up with the noise and begged a bit of peace. Their shop wasn't as big as ours, and Mrs. Farr ran it on her own when Mr. Farr had gone to work. She spent a lot of time talking to Mum in the afternoon, when they were "slack". Graham didn't go to Sunninghill School like us; he went to Pikes Lane which he could walk to, so he didn't have to catch the bus, which was a pity because the trolley buses fascinated him. I won't say he was a dunce, but he wasn't all that clever and liked to play with girls, which was a good job because most of the kids around us were girls. Dad used to say he was a bit of a jessy because he played with us, but he always stuck up for himself, even if he was outnumbered by girls. He was no pushover, often losing his temper when thwarted, flailing out with clenched fists in a sort of paddling movement and running off in a strop, with an "I'm going to tell my Mum of you", and he did, with her coming outside to sort us all out, then taking him in after we had all been chastised. The next day all would be forgotten when he came to call for us, because he

71

had no-one else to play with. We were all friends for years until they sold their shop and moved "up Deane". Mum and Mrs. Farr would often go dancing and jitterbugging to Bolton Palais, the big dance hall in town, togged up to the nines. The next day's talk would be peppered with whispers behind cupped hands, with lots of laughing, out of Dad's earshot. The shop wasn't much, just greengrocery and bits of stuff on a shelf behind the counter, but she did make and sell cracking ice-lollies: Vimto and turquoise spearmint, as well as a pink one that might have been sarsaparilla, only a penny each. Demand outstripped supply in the frantic rush on hot days; eventually they ceased to sell them after complaints from proper customers who couldn't get served in the crush.

Mostly we used to play in the back street, at Tipple Ups against the back wall of the mill, Hopscotch and Tig which was a chasing game, where you tigged someone by touching them. Then they had to be the chaser. That was made more difficult by being "safe" if off the ground, on a lamp post or a wall, anywhere your feet didn't touch the ground. We would also pester Dad over the back door until he threatened to chase us off or call the bobby. We played "Twoosie Ball" against Billy Pike's garage door, or a game of rounders if there were enough of us, if not cricket, being careful not to hit the ball too hard because of all the windows. We did manage to break a couple in our day, one in the mill and one of Dad's. He was none too pleased at the time, but it was an accident and not intentional. Broken windows were a serious offence, one which you could get a good hiding for from the window's owner, and your Dad if he found out. We missed the Farrs when they moved "up Deane", though they would always call in to see us on their way down to town to catch up on the neighbourhood gossip, but by then we were edging into our teens and had all got past playing out.

At the end of the block was the catering and hardware store owned by Mr. and Mrs. Hough. They lived away from the shop in a big house "up Heaton", the posh end of town. They had a teenage son and a daughter who had bright ginger hair and would come down to the shop in the school holidays and join in our games. She had a silly infectious giggle and went to dancing classes at the Dorrie Horne School of Dancing, who did the "Dinky Dots" at the Grand Theatre on Churchgate. Often Mum would give us some money to go and watch the shows, sitting in the gods, way above the stalls, watching out for Dorothy's bright hair as the girls tapped and twirled about the stage in colourful costumes. It wasn't very easy to pick out, despite its brightness, because we were so high up and far away. It's a wonder we didn't suffer from vertigo and altitude sickness. Still, it was a good six penn'orth in its day and kept us from under Mum's feet once a month. Dorothy's Mum, Mrs. Hough (Mum always called her Mrs. Hough), could probably have talked for England. She would come in just before teatime to pick up her loaf and regularly spend a good three quarters of an hour talking, so we all had to wait for our tea. Dad kept out of the way, clacking his fingers and nodding his head, as he "took them off"

73

gossiping about all and sundry. Mum would come in when she had finally gone, after more than one aborted attempt, and sit down with a thud, blowing out a gasp, as though out of breath with the ferociousness of it all. Eventually they came to live over the shop, and in the end there were only the two families, them and us, living on the premises in the whole of our block.

There were three houses around the corner, two in Mather Street and one in Edgar Street, all very old and run down. All were occupied by witches. Granny Powell and Miss Atherton, black witches both, lived in the small flagstone-floored hovels in Edgar Street. They looked about ninety, but were probably in their seventies, and would stand at their respective doors, beckoning us with toothless grins. We did our best to ignore them, being rather in awe of them, but in the end curiosity and guilt got the better of us and we would edge our way over to see what they wanted. More often it was a telling off for some minor offence like playing ball against their wall or making too much noise in the course of our play, but sometimes it was to ask us to run some errand to one of the little shops on the road. Occasionally it would prove profitable, but Mum didn't like us accepting money and we were supposed to say "Thank you, but it's all right" to anything offered, in the name of Mum's pride. With Granny Powell and Miss Atherton, it was usually a dash to the tobacco shop three blocks up near Magee's Brewery, for their usual quota of six penn'orth of snuff. We hated going, but they would look at us so pleadingly that we did, running back with the disgusting stuff to have it snatched out of our hands with the quick proffer of a coin and the door shut sharply in our faces. It was the only time they were ever nice to us, when they wanted something.

Cissie, who lived in Edgar Street, had a better house and was somewhat younger. Preferring a cross-over pinny and turban to the black shawl, she still wore the same ancient clogs. Being in our back street, she would complain constantly of our twoosie ball on her wall to Mum, and come to the door and raise her fists, shouting at the top of her voice, "Clear off, go and play somewhere else, you lot." The only time I remember any kindness from them all was when a tiny kitten strayed in and fell down their old tippler toilet in the back yard, shared by them all. They went to great lengths to get the poor terrified, bedraggled mite out, even to calling out the local bobby. We could hear its pitiful mewing as it was grabbed by the scruff of its neck and hauled out, to be dunked in a bowl of warm water to clean it up. Despite the double shock it did survive, but whose it was remained a mystery, and it ran off after downing a saucer of milk to revive it.

Across the road, facing our block, was the Progress Stores. A bazaar of sorts which sold everything from A to Z, it ran a club into which you paid your money every week, a sort of hire purchase in advance, because you paid for your goods before you got them. It was run by a Mr. Simon and Mr. Goldstone, who were Jewish. They sold clothes, hardware, toys, in fact anything they could stock on the premises. It was a wonderland, a sort of mini Woolworth's. They sold bouncy rubber balls and made a fortune out of us, when Dad wasn't talking to Billy Pike and we couldn't get our ball back. Walter Simms, one of the characters of Derby Street, who everybody will remember for his on-the-spot quotations of Shakespeare, was employed by them. A character and a half, he would return to Derby Street long after the Progress Stores had closed down to see all the friends he had made over the years, spending his days chatting to all and sundry up and down the area, with an opinion on anything and everything.

Next to the Progress Stores was the rooming house run by Mr. Cassidy, who let out rooms to the local "pros"; needless to say, it was a bit of a flea pit with Mr. Cassidy sitting outside, smoking a pipe, while the girls "entertained". We used to think he was part gypsy, a common sight in those days, when the fairs came, because he always wore a neckerchief and an earring in one ear. Agnes, one of his lodgers, was the local "bike", and although getting on in years she made a living. Dad used to snigger when he saw anyone going in, saying they would come out with more than they bargained for, and Mum, always nosey, would have eyes like "chapel hat pegs", looking to see if it was anyone who came into the shop. It all caused a bit of amusement one night when the bobby had to be sent for to break up a brawl. Luckily the police box was on the corner and the bobby nearby. The poor unfortunate was taken away as well as Agnes, because it was all illegal. Dad said he mustn't have had his money's worth, he'd kicked up such a fuss. Anyway, they were back in business after a while when the fuss had died down, much to everybody's amusement.

Mr. Pearson's was the next shop along, just across the road from us. A well-stocked grocer's, it was the local equivalent of Asda at the time, and was run by Mr. Pearson, who was very deaf, and his son John, who he bullied unmercifully. Mr. Pearson was also a widower and John was about sixteen or seventeen, with bright red curly hair. When he reached eighteen, he was called up to do his national service in the army, leaving Mr. Pearson to cope on his own. A quick errand for a tin of peas could take half an hour, he was so understaffed. Woe betide anyone with a list when the queue behind them stretched out of the small shop. Mum felt sorry for him. Being deaf herself, they had a lot in common and would shout to one another in sympathy while other people talked in normal voices, being unaware that there was a problem, deafness being invisible. Mum would cook him a dinner with ours, for John too when he was there, and would see us across the road with the covered plates, to hover at the back of his shop until he noticed us and took the plates into the back. She would then watch for us coming back and wave us across when it was safe. He was a nice man, despite his bullying of John, and the dinners must have been cold when he ate them but he never complained; he washed up the plates, and brought them back when he had shut the shop. Dad used to call him her boyfriend. No doubt about it, they got on famously. The dinners came to an end after about five years, when boredom with tinned peas, meat and potatoes set in, and John started coming across for one of Dad's pies.

Tinned peas, meat and potatoes was sometimes the limit of Mum's culinary expertise, especially when she was busy in the shop, but the less said about that the better. In later years a small rebellion and a bit of good humoured kidding put that right in the end. When we started cookery lessons at school, Mr. Pearson would weigh us an ounce of this and that without a blanch, and he had the patience of Job with us, even to asking how the dish had turned out, unaware of the sloshed-about mess we had brought home which Mum had promptly relegated to the dustbin once the kidding was over. We could always tell when he was in the shop by the high pitched whistling of his hearing aid, which was wired into a box on his chest. Needing constant adjustment, he happily went up and down the scales to reach a satisfying pitch, only to have to start again when a trolley bus went past. In later years, when Mum was told she needed a hearing aid, her first response was "not like Mr. Pearson's" and immediately went private, costly or not.

Mr. and Mrs. Mann had the local barber shop, sandwiched between Mr. Pearson's and the second paint and wallpaper shop, Mr. and Mrs. Proudfoot's. Mr. Mann was rather small and had a built-up shoe to make up for a six-inch deficiency in the length of one leg. I don't think it was a club foot, more of a birth deformity for which, in the days before the excellent orthopaedic surgery of today, not much could be done, apart from building up shoes to lengthen the limb. His wife was a very quiet sort, who fetched and carried to make up for his limited mobility. Clad in the ever-present cross-over pinny, she would help him in the shop, sweeping up the hair, gowning customers, shaving, and taking the money. She also tortured customers with a pair of very blunt hand clippers, a few minutes to savour at the end of a hair cut. There were two swivel chairs in the shop in front of a large mirror. Each was height-adjustable, and would be cranked up to suit his reach. Around each the lino was well worn with his constant to-ing and fro-ing, though this was not really noticeable as it was covered in hair. We would accompany Graham, when his Mum could bribe him into going, for his usual donkey fringe and short back and sides, to give him false courage and our support. Not one of his favourite outings. All three of us would sit there, waiting his turn and watching the show while Mr. Mann snipped and clunked around the chair in a flurry of activity, his exaggerated arm movements more like a ballerina than a barber. Graham dreaded the call to the chair and, cringing, he endured the next ten minutes with great fortitude, eyes tight shut as the donkey fringe was levelled, never an easy task, with his head imploded into his chest, Mrs. Mann hovering ready to swoop with the clippers. At last, neck brushed, gown whipped off, he would leap from the chair before it was lowered, with watery eyes and a huge grin of relief, to spend the next two hours with his hand down his back scratching. Still, his suffering was minimal compared to ours when we endured Mum's home perms, and no bribe was ever forthcoming.

Mrs. Proudfoot's was where Mum sent us to buy our paraffin for the tilly lamp she kept in the shop. A monstrosity of a thing, it required technical knowledge to light, a lot of prayer, and copious amounts of pumping the little brass handle that went in and out. She kept a medicine bottle of methylated spirits to put in the collar to start it off; not very wise; nor was the pop bottle of paraffin under the shop counter to top up the bottom bit. She sent us regularly across the road for paraffin, seeing us across when the traffic was clear, to enter the hall of the hallowed domain. It was a house really, and the shop was in one of the rooms down the hall, in which we were always supposed to wait until Mrs. Proudfoot served us. Often, Mrs. Proudfoot would be in the back, and we would have to open the front door to re-ring the bell several times before she appeared. It was always freezing, even in summer, a high lofty house with a stone tiled corridor, rather posh really. When she did finally appear, she would disappear again to fill the pop bottle, wipe it and take our half crown and, if feeling generous, see us back across the road. Mum, rubbing her hands and complaining we had been a long time, would then start her tussle with the tilly lamp, with a lot of "dratting" and "damn thing" emerging as she pumped away at the little brass handle that went in and out. It was an art to start it, but eventually it gave up the ghost and she threw it away. We certainly didn't miss our visits to Mrs. Proudfoot's cold little hall, and Mum certainly didn't miss the tussles with the tilly lamp, getting a new heater that was easy to light with a match.

80

In our close environment was also the mill in the back street. This gave us an interesting place to play, because it contained "the fire hole" where Adam continuously stoked the boilers that provided the steam to work the engines that whipped the looms backwards and forwards. Always a great source of fascination, the entrance to the fire hole was down a slope, the door at the bottom a great gaping no-go area from which we were chased at regular intervals. The three great shutter doors at the top of the back street were open in summer to alleviate the great heat the furnaces created, giving us insight into the workings of the mill, and this is where the vast amounts of coke were tipped regularly, forming huge piles in the three bays that housed it. Adam was a great mountain of a man who spent the majority of his time heaving great shovelfuls of coke into the vast furnaces, watched by all the kids who played in the back street and, of course, cheeked now and again by the more daring of us. Dad was friendly with him, but Billy Pike and Adam didn't get on very well, owing to the coke delivery wagons blocking the back street and the access to his garage, to which he seemed to demand access the minute they showed up. Usually, when they delivered, there was a pile of coke left in the back street, which had to be shovelled manually into the bays by Adam with an enormous spade. Neither was he a young man; he was into his sixties, with a great shock of white hair and a large stomach, kept regularly stoked with Dad's pies. They often used to chat in the back street, Adam with a pie in his hand delivered by Dad fresh from the oven, often with a cup of tea to keep down the dust that swirled around the place and choked everything. There was a constant procession at times to the pit at the top of the street, when the ashes were raked from the boilers and transported by Adam with the aid of a large wheelbarrow up a long plank to tip them on top of the pile, still warm from the furnace. This pit was a regular play area for us, running up the plank to jump on the retaining wall and leap off with a loud whoop to land on the cinders, making a loud crunch beneath our feet. It was also the main source of many a scabbed knee, and the need for Mum to keep in stock a large bottle of T.C.P. and a steady supply of plasters to stick on the scraped hands we acquired on landing. Despite the many bad landings, it was one of the most popular games of the back street, along with Pooh Sticks in the gutter water when Dad was swilling out.

The fire hole was a great source of amusement in other ways, because there was the cotton waste. Brought down in huge wicker skips, it was a tangle of cotton thread, spoil from the looms, I think, and Dad often used it to wipe out his pie tins. It was great stuff to throw at one another if left unattended for any length of time, as long as we picked up the stuff and put it back in the skips that were left at the top of the slope.

One of Dad's favourite haunts on Derby Street, once we had a car, was Britannia Garage, which was just down the road towards Deane Road. It was run by a man called Alf Martin, from what I can remember. He was a real help to Dad when he first was struggling with a car that was a real tartar to keep running. Many was the time we were sent down with a plug or two to sandblast, running back with the cleaned up plugs, and holding our breath while he turned the starting handle, hoping the engine would burst into life. We knew that if it wouldn't we would be sent back at the double to ask Alf to come up and tinker in the back street until it did. Poor Alf was never away sometimes, especially if Dad had deliveries to make. He must have dreaded our appearance in his forecourt with the messages and the damp plugs. Britannia Garage was the old type of garage, with just a few petrol pumps and a workshop on the side. When all else failed, and Alf Martin declared a new part was needed, it was a family outing to Valentines, the scrap yard on Manchester Road, where we would peruse the old wrecked cars for a Morris Twelve like Dad's and dismantle a similar part, climbing over the wrecks trying to identify a likely candidate. We definitely enjoyed these outings, where Dad could obtain a cheap replacement part, although we were often shouted at by Mum, with Dad too getting into trouble for all the oil on our clothes. When the Suez crisis was in full swing, motorists queued up past our shop to fill up with petrol. Dad thought it was great, because our trade increased. There was a lot of jocular talk with Alf Martin at the time, and when the crisis was over they were both better off. Who says an ill wind does nobody any good?

This then was our little neighbourhood, where most of the families I have mentioned lived behind their shops. None of them made a fortune out of them, and did not expect to, but all of them made a living. They provided an interesting community for us to grow up in. Some of course disappeared over the years, and were sadly missed, like Mr. and Mrs. Farr; others died, like Mr. Costello. Others, like Mr. and Mrs. Pike, moved up and away into better living accommodation. All in all, the times changed in the 1960s, leaving us somewhat isolated at times, and eventually Mum and Dad too moved away to live in a bungalow, but that was in the early 1970s after more than twenty years of living behind the shop.

CHAPTER
FIVE

Round and About

Bolton in the late 1940s and 1950s was a very different place from the multiracial place of the present day. Comprising a multitude of terraced streets, every locality was more or less self-contained. There were hundreds of little shops, even in people's homes where a front room sufficed as a business premises for an enterprising family. Most were on corners of streets, and known as such-a-body's corner shop, where neighbours could be sure of a bit of company and a good gossip, and there was a chair placed in the corner for the unsteady or those suffering from a shortage of puff. No doubt that was caused by the fluff, always in the air of the cotton spinning and weaving sheds, which would eventually wreck their lungs. Many of these little shops did tick — that's credit in modern day language, written up in a book and settled at the end of the week. Mum did it for a while, because it was expected, until she got stung a time or two, then a card went up in the window to say goods had to be paid for in full.

The streets across the road lived like that. John Street and James Street, and a maze of terraced streets named after the disciples in the Bible. When we acquired bikes, these were the streets it was safe to ride in, wheeling them across the road into the cobbled streets behind the Progress Stores where the ruts and potholes provided deep puddles to ride through after a shower of rain. In summer, they also provided a good supply of tar bubbles to pop when it was hot, and we could sit on the kerbs, free from the danger of traffic in our play. Dad garaged his car there as well, in one of a row of falling-down wooden garages, on a large piece of land that was a bomb site from the war, giving us all a break from the access rows with Billy Pike, which had become all too regular. Dad liked a peaceful life, really, and would go and tinker in peace with Reg in the next garage, who knew a bit about cars. Mum would send us across at regular intervals to remind him to come home when she thought he had been there long enough. Often, on the weekends when car repairs were deemed necessary, we were sent to tell him his dinner was in the oven and had been there for the past hour. Sometimes we took it across between two plates, like Mr. Pearson's, to eat in the middle of the on-going repairs, which were all-important to Dad, Mum giving up on him altogether with a shake of her head.

Between Derby Street and Deane Road, it was just one big maze really, all the way up to Smethhurst Lane off Daubhill where there were some green fields. It really was built up. In summer we would roam the area during the six week holidays. Mum hardly ever saw us, only when we were hungry. Then we would dash back, begging a pasty or a cake from the window, friends in tow, which Mum would often complain about, and then off back out to carry on the play until we were hauled in for our tea when Mum had shut the shop.

We were always filthy when we came in, Bolton being an industrial place, and us being kids. Always filthy. Sitting on the kerb, feet in the gutter, crawling on all fours to play marbles. Mum would gasp in exasperation when she saw us, and many was the time we were dragged in and made to sit still on the settee for half an hour, as a punishment for getting in that state. Then being taken upstairs one at a time to have our faces, hands and knees scrubbed roughly with a loofah, sitting on the edge of the bath silently as she lectured us, before being turned out to play again with the dire warning to stay clean. I remember vividly to this day the smell of Bolton dirt, but I can say, honestly, that we never came to much harm from it.

Often we played in the cinder pit at the top of the back street, begging some of Mum's bags and a scoop out of the bake house to ladle the cinders into the bags. Pretending they were chips, sprinkling them with pretend vinegar, and then wrapping them in newspaper, we played "chip shop", one of our favourite games when the level of the cinders was low, and the brick retaining wall made a "counter" from which to "serve". The cinders would get between our toes, even through our socks, and Dad would look out to find us all lined up, sitting on the kerb with our socks off, picking the cinders from between our toes. Needless to say our socks were filthy, and Dad, with a hoot of laughter and a "hey up", would pretend Mum was coming, at which we would hide them, delaying the telling off we knew was coming our way when she saw them. Eventually they would finish up grey, as all our white cotton socks did. It couldn't be avoided.

It wasn't only the socks that suffered. The toes of our shoes also came to grief in the efforts to climb the mill wall that kept the mill lodge from our view. Situated behind an eight foot wall, the lodge was out of bounds to all but the hardy. Not only was it behind an eight foot wall, that wall had a row of broken glass across the top in the effort to keep out inquisitive children, who often came to their deaths in the mill lodges of the area. Not only was swimming in their rubbish strewn depths dangerous, they also contained weed to tangle around the legs of unsuspecting children, dragging them down into their murky depths, a danger Mum made us very aware of. Hollis's Mill lodge was a source of fascination because it was so out of view. A climb up the stone wall, with the help of a leg up, just gave enough glimpse of the forbidden territory to warrant a roar of approval for our daring. The wall was just about climbable, with the jutting stone giving ample footholds, but the broken glass on top did deter any further incursion and so did the shout of any adult in the vicinity, who knew of the dangers, to "gid art of it".

Edgar Street was a good street to play in and, despite the occasional large lorries which sometimes came to Mitchell's engineering works, provided a good smooth surface for our roller skates when we acquired them. The workers from the mill used the street and piece of spare land opposite as a recreation ground in their dinner break to play rounders. With lots of kidding and flirting going on between the sexes, these games were a constant source of amusement, and drew a large audience to watch the horseplay in progress until the mill hooter went to spoil the fun and they all trooped back in for the afternoon's work. We were never stuck for something to do, and once the dinnertime rounders were over, which we always watched, another amusement took its place.

As we got older we went further afield, to Barrow Bridge and Moss Bank Park, where there was a zoo of sorts. Deane Brook held a lot of attraction for us, a narrow shallow brook, winding its way through Bolton to join up with the River Croal, and eventually the River Irwell, which flows through Manchester. We caught tadpoles and sloshed about in the mud in our wellies, making believe we were "up the Amazon" in the deepest jungle, our imagination soaring as we trampled in the flat banks of bulrushes on the sides of the stream. Eventually one of us would come to grief and fall in, our Wellington boots caked with the thick mud and held fast in the shallows, pulled out with a squelch and cleaned up with a bit of grass for the journey home in a disgraceful state. Then, chastised and kept in, cleaned up once more, before being sent back out to do it all again, with not a care in the world and chastisement forgotten. We had lots of imagination, and all the usual fall-outs and fights, us, Graham Farr and the Rickabys but they were soon forgotten.

The Rickabys were a family on the next block. They had a shop of sorts where they sold second-hand clothes and household items, various odds and ends, a bit of a mish-mash really. They had four children, well — three and a bump really when we knew them. Stuart arrived later and tagged along when he was old enough. Sheila, the eldest, was hoping to be a dancer and was a good bit older than us, so we didn't see much of her. Beverly was a couple of years older than us, had red hair and was covered in freckles. Bobby was our age. Beverly went to Derby Street School, across the road from their shop. I think it was segregated then, and if we stood on the wall, we could just about see in to shout for Beverly at dinnertime. Beverly was our ring leader when she played with us, and she was our pass out of Derby Street. Mum would let us go further afield if Beverly was with us because she was older. Taking jam butties and Spanish pop, we would set off for picnics at various parks. Queens Park was always our favourite, because it wasn't too far and had swings and a paddling pool, not like Bobby Haywards Park, which was a bit drab, the small playground being rather tame, and not having a climbing frame like Queens Park.

We spent all day there when the weather was good, playing on the climbing frame and on the two roundabouts Beverly would spin them very fast. We always ate the jam butties around the paddling pool, then gave the crusts to the ducks, playing hide and seek in the big banks of rhododendron bushes and spying on courting couples, giggling when they shouted at us to "Push off" when we asked them what time it was in the effort to interrupt the proceedings, knowing full well that they knew as well as us you could see the town hall clock from the park. But we were just curious, as most kids are. No-one would bother us, we were never frightened, even at dusk, as you would be now. Sometimes Mum would stump up the bus fare to Barrow Bridge, and we would walk down to Trinity Street to catch the next bus. We would dam the stream and play in the pool it made, a popular game to all children in the summer holidays.

It was a paradise then, a local beauty spot, and the houses along the stream had little wooden footbridges to them, as indeed they do today. Then, quite a few of them had little tea gardens with wooden benches where you could sit and have a cup of tea and a buttered scone or toasted teacake. Some sold homemade ice cream and bottles of pop, and there was a little shop that sold coltsfoot rock, that we always bought because it was very hot, making sure we had enough money left for the bus home, because it was quite a way to walk. Down near the bus stop, there was a small lake with a few rowing boats for hire. It was always a toss-up whether or not to spend any remaining money on the boats, or whether to have a ride on the swing boats at the side of the lake. Usually the swing boats won because they were cheaper, and we weren't very good at keeping the rowing boat straight, causing the boat man to shout from the bank and eventually to haul us in for safety's sake.

When Mum and Dad went, we got to go on both, but that was on a Sunday and Dad could row, with Mum watching from the bank because she wasn't too keen on boats or water. Today it is regarded as a posh part to live in Bolton, with the houses with little bridges over the stream being highly sought after, with their pretty little gardens being private and not catering for the likes of us. Many people like us must have many happy memories of Barrow Bridge in those days, and how it used to be, and the simple pleasures we enjoyed there as children. On days of rain, when trips to Barrow Bridge and forays "Up the Amazon" of Deane Brook were curtailed, we would don wellies and macs and explore the cavernous depths of Bolton Town Hall, plumbing the aquarium's watery world in the basement where we would seek out the Moray eel lurking in the weed at the bottom of its limited kingdom, then racing up the great swathe of stone staircase curving either side of the impressive entrance hall, to the natural history museum on the first floor, to stand gazing transfixed at the poor stuffed animals, their glassy eyes, brown and beadlike, following us as we trailed around the room. Stopping at the great bear, an enormous thing towering over us, we stared up at it, admiring its teeth and claws, yellow with age.

Many a wet afternoon was spent in here, and we never tired of it, often eyed with mistrust by the curator whose eyes bore some resemblance to the poor stuffed animals. His beady stare daring us to misbehave, he followed us around the rooms of exhibits, poring with dismay over our finger marks all over his glass cabinets kept hopelessly immaculate with his polishing cloth and feather duster.

Then it was off to the Egyptian room to take in the sarcophagi, standing on tiptoes to peer into the rotting layers of bandages at the poor mummy, now a shrunken mess of brown gunge at the bottom of a coffin in a glass cabinet displaying its once well-upholstered body at its worst, years after it had died. The bright lights of the museum picked out the entire imperfections the long-dead soul had sought to cover in the many layers of bandages and had hoped to preserve in the privacy of its tomb, only to be dragged out for us to poke gruesome fingers at in the silence of the museum on a wet day when we had little else to do. Despite the gruesome exhibits in the glass coffins, there were some fascinating relics as we moved from case to case, taking in the head of Nefertiti with its bright colours shining under the lights, and other old and crumbling things that, like us, had come in out of the rain and were dripping water on to the parquet floor, much to the dismay of the poor curator who had by now rectified the glass cabinets and was in further search of perfection.

Next it was the Art room to peruse the naked nymphs and plonk our bottoms on the island seating, soon becoming bored and racing down the staircase once more to hunt the elusive Moray eel in the basement. Becoming noisy, we were eventually persuaded to leave by the stern face of the door attendant and hunger. Then it was off for a packet of crisps and a hunt for the little blue bag of salt that always hung back at the very bottom of the packet.

Our trips to the children's library were quieter on the whole. There was no danger of boredom either, choosing a book to read at the little round tables and chairs where we were left in peace to read in the quiet surroundings. An Enid Blyton was a must, the J.K. Rowling of the day, and we followed the Famous Five, the Secret Seven, and all the adventures of Jack and Philip, Dinah and Lucy-Ann, waiting for Bill Smugs to show up, which he always did, to rescue them all and Kiki from some ultimate danger involving spies or criminals. Mum made sure we were readers as we grew older by refusing to have a television, so many a winter night was spent reading, with three pennyworth of sweets, in front of the fire, engrossed in a book until Dad would come out a with quip about something, and laughter would end the reverie. Mum would round it off by making the Horlicks and packing us off to bed.

Some nights we went to the pictures, walking down in a foursome, Mum and Dad linking with one of us on either side, rushing after tea to get in before the queue. As it was a continuous programme, we always managed at the time we went to get in part way through the film, seeing the middle and the end first and then the beginning when the programme started again, with the second feature and Pathé News in between, before the beginning started again. All very complicated, and it played havoc with the plot. But we could stay in to watch it through again if it was a good film. No-one threw you out; you could go in when they opened and stay till they closed as some old scruffy men with no homes often did. It was a hang-out haven for them, as we sometimes found to our cost. In the interval, before the main feature, the usherette appeared with the tray. It was quite cheap in those days, so we would all have a choc ice or a lolly, after an argument about who had to go to get them. The lollies were Orange Maids which left your tongue a bright orange, and we compared tongues until the programme started again.

Occasionally, very occasionally, as a special treat, Dad would let us have our tea in one of the cinema restaurants, served to us by a waitress properly attired in black dress, white frilly apron and cap, which was a head band with a frill. It was always served with a flourish as we sat in hushed awe minding our manners, with elbows off the table, juggling with the heavy "silver" cutlery and crisp white napkins on the white embossed table linen. Not daring to spill a drop of tea or gravy, we sat demure in the hushed atmosphere, feeling like we were undergoing a great occasion, wishing we could live so "posh" all the time despite having to watch our Ps and Qs. Dad dug deep into his wallet to pay while we went to the toilet, all three of us, and then on these occasions all went into the circle, the very best seats, making like we were wealthy. But as I say, it was a special treat given only occasionally. Most times we sat in the stalls, dodging sideways and forwards to see around people's heads for a clear view.

There were three such cinemas in Bolton that were in the plush zone and had restaurants. One was the ABC Capitol on Churchgate opposite the Grand Theatre, which was where we went to see the Dinky Dots on Saturdays. The others were the Odeon in Ashburner Street, and the Lido on Bradshawgate. The Odeon was very good with red velour plush seats; it had an organ that came up out of the orchestra pit at the interval. The Capitol was the furthest away from home, and after the show the long walk home proved to be a bit of a drag, especially in winter, so it had to be a good film to merit the walk. The Lido was the one we sometimes got complimentary tickets for. Mum and Dad knew the manager there, Mr. Fielding, who bought his bread from us. We would see him standing to attention in the foyer, done up in best evening suit which Dad always called his monkey suit, overseeing the queue and box office. He was quite friendly and would always wink a knowing wink, understanding how much we appreciated the tickets. Mum often reciprocated with a bit of free left-over stuff that wouldn't keep to sell the next day put in his order.

The Lido eventually became Bolton's only surviving cinema, and the one large screen became three studio cinemas, with the main screen in the circle and the rear stalls divided into two. The restaurant disappeared altogether long before that when television kept people away, closing the majority of Bolton's flea-pits too. The flea-pits were the local picture houses, and there were lots of them in Bolton in the 1950s. In our area alone we had the Tivoli, the Ritz, the Regent, the Majestic, and the Windsor. Not far away there were the Queens, the Carlton, the Belle, and the Palace. Some eventually went to bingo, but mostly television finished them off. At sometime or another we went to every one but generally the Tivoli, where they had the Saturday children's show, usually every Saturday. We went with Graham as a rule, walking up, looking at the chimpanzee in the pet shop on the way. The chimp was often on a chain outside and sometimes in its cage in the shop. It was very tame but kept in strict control. We saw it pull a little boy up against the cage once. It was only curious, but after that it was kept away from children, because the poor little boy's Mum said it was dangerous. It put us off it a bit, I must say, and we kept well away, out of its reach, but we still went to see it. Another shop that fascinated us up there was the Chinese Laundry, because after watching all the Saturday serials in which the villains always seemed to be Chinamen, we steered well clear of them on our way home. Often, after a visit to the Tivoli, Mum would have to cut chewing gum out of our hair. It was somewhat of a nuisance, that and the lighted matches that were occasionally thrown in the excitement of the moment. Despite all that, it never put us off going, and it was a regular Saturday morning thrill during which we joined in the feet stamping and shouting along with the rest.

We often went to the pictures three times a week, either with Mum and Dad or on our own. Of course they attracted the perverts in the afternoons, and often we had to move seats several times because of the "Knee-nudgers", who draped themselves onto us despite the presence of the usherettes who regularly shone their torches down the rows in the pretence of looking for empty seats. These men were probably a source of complaints and well-known to them, but they never seemed to be thrown out. We always tried to sit next to a woman if possible, then it didn't happen; other than that we just had to keep moving. The front row of the circle was best, where there was plenty of leg room and no perverts, but those were the dear seats. So often when it was dark we would get up and go to the toilet, coming back to sit in the circle. No-one ever noticed, or asked to see your ticket once the show had been going a bit. The usherettes were all at the back of the stalls, gossiping, and smoking until the lights went up for the interval and the ice cream trays came out. Despite our tender ages we had it all sussed; we had to have, or we would have been molested.

When the Queen was crowned in 1952, we were taken by the school to watch the film of the ceremony made in glorious Technicolor. That was an experience, being marched down to the Odeon in a crocodile of pairs, holding hands to keep us in some kind of control, down the whole of Derby Street, the whole school in class order with the teachers supervising at intervals. What a sight we must have been, waving to Mum in the shop as we passed by. Being so young it was a bit wasted on us, and most of us became bored in the middle, shuffling about in our seats. Thankfully, after what seemed like hours, it ended and we all filed out again, back up Derby Street to write about it and draw a picture, and be given a coronation mug with the Queen's head on it. We had them quite a while but eventually, as most did, they got broken and put in the bin.

When we finished school (at four o'clock in those days), we would play in the back street until tea-time, calling for Graham as soon as he was home from Pikes Lane. Mum would call us in for our tea when she had shut the shop. Usually it was bread and butter, with

Dad's potted meat paste or Shippam's spread which, by the amount of it we ate in our childhood, must have kept their profits in high order well into the 1960s. Once our tea was thrown down, it was back out to play until we had to be literally dragged in, thrown in the bath or scrubbed with the loofah, depending on the amount of dirt we had collected. Then, still protesting at the unfairness of it all, we were tucked into bed.

Summer play was the best. Tar bubbles, forming between the cobbles in the hot sun, were swooped on with glee, and we often walked home from school, spending the bus fare on a lolly, walking down the back streets to avoid all the bobbies, with lolly in hand, one forefinger black with tar, jumping the nicks in the flags where the devil might come up to snatch us down in to Hell. We were full of these sorts of fears, instilled in us by old wives' tales and Mum and Granny, in the effort to keep us "good" little girls when we stood at the gates of Heaven waiting to be let in. We always gave the bobbies a wide berth anyway. They were a scourge we were threatened with on many an occasion, either that or Edgeworth Homes, the local children's orphanage Mum would threaten to send us to when we were naughty. We always believed her too. Her many threats to "run away with a black man" didn't ring true, though, because there were none around us, only the engineers at Mitchell's in Edgar Street whose faces were black with dirt.

In winter, there was always the hope of snow and any cold snaps brought with them an excitement in the anticipation of it. We would whoop with glee at the first sight of it, falling over one another in the rush to find our wellies in the glory hole under the stairs, disregarding any fear of the odd lurking cockroach which usually inhibited our excursions there. Once clad in warm clothes, it was out to make slides, trampling the snow into a hard crust and rubbing it with the soles of our wellies until it gleamed in the dim lamplight of the evening back street. We were often told off by the old witches for making the pavement dangerous, but then would find our much-prized slide mushy and melted with salt the following day. The snow soon went black with all the dirt, but we always managed a snowman or two and once, when a heavy snowfall closed the schools for a day or so, made a huge igloo out of large blocks, only to find it fallen in the next morning, the dirt and cinders from the spare land, where we had cut the blocks, adhering to the mushy mess. We would play until our fingers and feet were frozen; the pain of them thawing out in front of the open fire and the resulting chilblains from this made us cry with despair, and sent Mum running down to Mr. Costello's for the chilblain ointment to soothe and shrink them back to normal again.

In those days we would shovel the snow from the front of the shop. Everyone did, heaping it into huge piles in the road. Those who were unable to, like Mr. Costello, were usually helped, Mum often sending us down to do the job for him with the coal shovel and a brush. He was always grateful, and gave us a glass of hot Vimto each in gratitude. It was expected of everyone to move the snow from their own shop front

100

and to salt it to keep it from freezing. People were more considerate of others to a certain extent, and each did their bit.

Eventually we were all glad when the snow went, for it became black very quickly in Bolton's dirty atmosphere, leaving great piles of black crusty mounds in the road. Bolton wasn't a clean air zone as it is today. Everyone had coal fires belching smoke as well as the mill chimneys around us, and the smuts in the atmosphere had to be seen to be believed. White washing was brought in dotted with smuts to Mum's never-ending dismay, leaving her shaking her head with an "It's a mucky hole is this" as she inspected the washing from the backyard. Hung in two lines, from window to coke hole and back to the other side of the window, we often had to duck under it to get to the toilet and back. With Dad's constant stoking of the bakehouse oven and boiler, it was often finger-marked as well. In the damp days of October and November, thick pea souper fogs were commonplace. They were so thick and dense with smoke and smuts you could taste them. On venturing out for any length of time, our nostrils became black from breathing the dire stuff, leaving a smudge of black dirt under our noses and on our top lips. No doubt it accounted for a lot of deaths at that time of year, it was so bad.

Many of the old folk, who had worked as spinners and weavers in the cotton mills all their lives, succumbed to it. Being vulnerable, and with their lungs damaged by the fluff, the fogs just finished them off. Many people were aware of the dangers and covered their faces with scarves, but it still got through and the taste of it seemed to linger for days. Often the buses would stop running, their drivers being unable to see where they were going and refusing to carry on. Once while I was coming home from school, the bus-conductor walked in front of the bus all the way down Derby Street and back to the depot, it was so dangerous. Even we as passengers couldn't see far enough to know where to get off, and were taken into town where we had to walk back the two stops to our home. In later years Mum would take her washing to the local wash house, where it was washed, dried and ironed, and brought home without smuts.

Despite the smuts, she carried on for now, using the small Hoover washer with fold down hand-wringers, kept in the corner of the kitchen. It was only about eighteen inches square, and thirty inches deep, which she filled with hot water. A little wheel in the side swooshed it all round, entangling the clothes in the process. A pair of laundry tongs were needed to untangle it all, steaming from the tub, then it was wrung through the rubber rollers, one hand grappling with the tongs because it was all hot while the other hand turned the handle, guiding the washing up into the sink. It was all very technical in its day and, despite the tangling, washed the clothes clean. The rinsing was very wet and messy, as was the several wringings needed to get out all the water, and the kitchen floor was always swimming at the end of it all. It then had to be put onto the washing lines in the yard, with a threat to watch the weather. We dreaded it all. Not that it affected us that much, but she was always somewhat tetchy until it was done, with the many interruptions to see to the shop. Despite the many wringings, it dripped in the yard for hours and was finished off on the rack over the fire, pulled up and down by a rope secured to a hook in the wall, in winter dangling over our heads as we toasted our developing corned beef legs and chilblains in front of the fire.

Bedding was a job on its own, as it was flannelette in winter and smooth cotton in summer, both difficult to dry. Blankets were only washed occasionally as they tended to mill up, being wool, and the eiderdowns not at all. When Mrs. Hough moved in over their shop, she and Mum decided to go to the wash house together. It was in Rothwell Street, one of the side streets off Derby Street, not far up the road, and they would happily trot off together with an old pram full of dirty washing as soon as it opened, and be back at their shops to open at nine o'clock with washing done, dried and ironed on the big steam roller press, full of local gossip gained in the process to be passed on eagerly to Dad and distributed with the bread, pies and cakes to regular customers, with a lot of laughing and cheeky talk if it involved the latest goings on at the brothel across the road.

Lily Horrocks, the sister of Ada, the local hairdresser, often joined them. She lived around the corner in Fletcher Street, with son Jackie who wasn't quite a full shilling. Their yard backed onto our back street, forming the cul-de-sac at the top end of Edgar Street. Jackie hung around watching us play, but didn't join in.

He was kept on a tight rein, to protect him from the taunts of other kids, I suppose. We liked him, and when he grew up he would talk to Mum in the shop. Mum being deaf didn't always understand him, frustrating him no end in the effort to get his point across. There were other children who, like Jackie, didn't join in our play. Ada's daughter, Jackie's cousin, was one. Nina was always a dainty little thing, chubby, and dark haired, and always immaculate in a pretty dress. She occasionally played with us, but not often. Barbara Smethurst, who lived on the next block, was another. She once locked us in her Dad's garage and wouldn't let us out, so she wasn't very popular after that. One girl who often appeared in our back street in the summer holidays was very different to the rest. Mum said she was an albino. She had snow-white hair and pink eyes, which she crinkled up in the light. She came to her Grandma's in Carey Street. Her Grandad was the night watchman in the mill at the back. We knew her Grandma, because she trundled up the back street regularly with a jug of ale covered by a tea towel, from the Peacock in Great Moor Street. They would drink it by the fire hole door sitting on two chairs, on summer nights when we played in the back street. Ann was at boarding school, and also had a young brother with the same pink eyes, They got teased quite a bit because of the pink eyes, but they were real scrappers when it came down to it; fists flying, they knew how to defend themselves. They were always nicely dressed when they arrived, but as the days went by Carey Street took over, and they finished up like the rest of the ragamuffins who lived there, dirty and unkempt. They disappeared eventually, and Carey Street was knocked down, leaving a flat, brick-strewn, empty space. We often wondered what happened to them, as we rode our bikes through the puddles. We even missed the odd half brick being thrown at us by the Carey Street gang. No doubt they were throwing bricks at some other kids somewhere; it was a way of life to them nothing would ever stop.

Eventually the two houses in Mather Street were pulled down too. Both Annie Atherton and Granny Powell died, and shortly afterwards Cissie's house was pulled down to make way for a garage. Even the horse trough from which we rescued many a drowning fly in summer disappeared too, no longer needed when all the horses were retired and lorries took their place. We missed the horses and the carts that ploughed up Derby Street to Magee's Brewery. They were a familiar sight, the dray carts loaded with great barrels of ale. We would often stand watching the draymen roll the barrels down into the cellars of the pubs nearby, holding the reins and stroking the great big carthorses' necks. Mum would give us a bit of bread or a barm cake, to hold in the palm of our hand while they nuzzled it into their soft velvet mouths. They were very gentle creatures, responding well to their drivers' "whoa" when they edged their way slightly up the street. It wasn't quite the same when the lorries took over, and the manure in big steaming heaps in the road wasn't there to be quickly shovelled into a sack for the allotments by some enterprising gardening Grandad. Dad had his flour delivered by horse and cart for quite a while too, once causing quite a stir when the horse got quite frisky and finished up at the top of the street, flour wagon included, in the dead end. Eventually it had to be unharnessed to turn the wagon around. We all stood watching as the poor drover and Dad dragged the cart around in the confines of the back street.

Many of the streets across the road also started to be demolished in the general slum clearance of the mid-1950s, changing our neighbourhood quite a bit and leaving great flat open spaces. Dad lost some of his customers too, as they were moved to the new council estates being built further out of town in Great Lever and Breightmet. Gradually great blocks of houses around us changed into open spaces, leaving the way open for the caravans of travelling people to set up camp. They proved to be a great nuisance to us for a time as their children ran riot, begging in the shop for stale bread and jerry cans of water. Most were scrap dealers, and anything that wasn't nailed down in the area disappeared. They were a very enterprising lot, and often the police turned up to help when the council was brought in to move them on. After a continuous stream of them on the flattened land all around us, a bulldozer turned up one day to heap up the earth into a barrier to keep them off. We who were left living in the properties still standing heaved a big sigh of relief; the council must have heaved a sigh of relief too, because they weren't easy to get rid of, once encamped.

CHAPTER
SIX

Granny

When school broke for the long summer holidays at the end of July, Mum would pack us off to Granny's for two weeks. I don't know whether it was for our benefit, for the fresh air as opposed to the smoke, or to give Mum and Dad a break, or company for Granny. Grandad had died when we were about seven, leaving Granny missing him deeply. We went to see him when he was ill in bed upstairs in the little front bedroom. He was obviously very poorly and weak, not having very long to live, and Granny was crying in the living room when we came down, Mum and Dad comforting her. We didn't see him again, and Mum and Dad went to his cremation, leaving us with Grandma Toothill and Susan and Ann, feeling we were too young to attend. After that, when we all went to Horsforth, it was very sad for a time, and Granny came to stay with us in Bolton more often, sleeping in the back bedroom with us. We had lovely holidays with Granny, and enjoyed the country lanes around which were sadly lacking in our town environment, though Mum and Dad would take us out in the evenings in the better days of summer when the shop closed, catching the bus to Montserrat to walk across the golf links, taking the moorland road, then the footpath down to the 99 steps, and on down to Barrow Bridge. Sometimes Mr. and Mrs. Farr and Graham would join us, all laughing and chatting as we walked, ending up at Bob's Smithy, sitting on the pub steps with a glass of lemonade while the grownups indulged in something stronger inside before emerging to catch the bus home. It was a pleasant walk on a nice summer evening, and we could see over the whole of Bolton and count all the mill chimneys, picking out the ones near home. Most of them have gone now, as most of the cotton mills closed and were demolished to make way for housing and the industrial estates which followed. Later, when Dad bought his first car, we would all manage to pile into the car and leave Bolton behind to seek the countryside further afield.

Our summer holidays with Granny were absolute magic, and our stay with her was looked forward to with great relish. Mum and Dad would deliver us, very excited and with our small suitcase of clothes. Mum and Granny would make a great show of the issue of our keep, with money being pushed backwards and forwards, Granny refusing to take it and Mum refusing to have it back. It was eventually slipped on to the sideboard quietly by Mum when she thought Granny wasn't looking, only to be spotted and the whole argument begun again. It was a matter of pride to them both and very often was rather silly as Granny was poorer than us. Somehow or another it was always left, and Granny made the pretence of being livid when it was discovered slipped in some corner, but she must have been glad of it, because the fresh air gave us big appetites for Granny's home baking, and kept her constantly at the rolling pin when we were there.

When it was time for them to leave, there was a lot of kissing and threats to be good as we waved them off at the end of the street, waving until they disappeared into the distance. Then feeling rather lost and forlorn, and keeping a stiff upper lip, we helped Granny put our clothes into the chest of drawers, sniffing at the mothballs with wrinkled noses. Granny always used mothballs, they were in all the drawers, much to our distain, and our clothes often smelled of them when we went home much to Dad's amusement. Granny's back bedroom had a strange smell I can remember to this day. It was a smell of dust and polish combined with the faint musty smell of the mothballs emanating from the deep drawers of the heavy old oak furniture. That first night we were always upset. Missing Mum and Dad and shedding a tear or two, we huddled in the big double bed, Granny coming to kiss us goodnight and give us a hug before her ablutions, knowing we would be sad. Our tears were washed away in the first light of the following day as we awoke to our holiday and sought our playmates in Rose Avenue, Mum and Dad forgotten in the rush outside to play. The bedroom had a sash window, the lower half covered by a heavy cream lace curtain, through which the sun would stream on to our faces as we woke, if we were lucky. Granny's bedroom was at the front, down a narrow landing at the top of the spiralling stairs. Further along, the other way, was another straight staircase leading up to the attic, its door always closed to keep out the draught from the small skylight in the roof.

This room contained all sorts of fascinating paraphernalia and tin trunks, in which were kept old clothes and the things she couldn't bring herself to throw away. One such item was Joey's cage. Joey was a green budgerigar which Mum and Auntie Phyllis had had before the war. He was a much-loved family pet and apparently very talkative. Granny would regale us with his sayings and, although we had never seen him, we felt we knew him as well as Granny. He flew away to freedom one day from Mum's shoulder as she took the ashes to the dustbin, breaking all their hearts when they couldn't tempt him back into the house. Granny could never bring herself to throw his cage away, neither could she bear to have another budgie, and the empty cage was put in the attic where it remained for years. We could never go into the attic without lifting out the cage, and picturing the little green budgie in it. Despite its disappearance from all their lives, its memory remained as well as the cage amid all the junk in the attic.

Sometimes, when Mum and Dad stayed at Granny's instead of at Grandma Toothill's as they usually did, Granny would make us a bed up on the floor of the attic in amongst the trunks and things long since done with. We always loved that, peering about to see what we could spot that we hadn't discovered before. There was always something, it was such a wonderland, the morning light from the little skylight picking out the dim corners and the old boxes full of old-fashioned things. Once wakened and the discovering done, we would creep down the steep attic steps to Mum and Dad in the small bedroom we occupied in summer, and into bed with them like we did at home to be warmed up again, our feet freezing from the cold attic floor. In summer Granny would put a bolster down the middle of the bed to keep us apart. Fights often broke out between us when one of us hogged the middle of the bed. Kicks and fists were used in the effort to establish our space. It usually ended in tears, with Granny dashing up to re-establish a workable peace, digging out the bolster to mark a boundary down the middle of the bed. Being in a flock bed, we tended to roll into the middle anyway, Jean, I and the bolster. Despite all the arguments of the previous night, we never held a grudge, and were best of friends, if somewhat wary of one another, the following morning.

Granny's bed had a feather mattress which needed to be shaken every day to fluff it up. Each holding a corner and Granny two, we would all shake like fury on the count of three, until the feathers were evenly distributed. Then we would smooth over the top and bottom sheet and pick up any feathers floating around the room from the vigorous shaking, chasing them into the corners as they floated away from our eager fingers and sharp sneezes from all the dust. Eventually this mattress would end up in Bolton along with the sprung platform and bedstead when she came to stay with us, Dad putting it together in our bedroom where we would all sleep. Her nightly ablutions were a revelation to us, as she took off her corset and pink Celanese

111

bloomers, and downed the nightly glass of senna pods, a lifelong habit to keep her "regular". We watched the morning ritual as she put the pods in a glass of boiling water to steep, ready to be drunk the last thing before she went to sleep. They were a bit of a fascination to us and we had to sniff them each day out of childish curiosity, slyly dipping in a finger to taste occasionally as the bitter drink was stirred and left to cool on the dressing table next to the bed. It certainly did keep her regular, and she was often in the toilet when we all wanted to "go". The one toilet was not sufficient at times for the five of us and Mum and Dad's staff, when the doses of "Syrup of Figs" were meted out to us as well, as was Mum's regular habit. Granny joined in with the "Toilet Humour" of Mum and Dad, shrieking with laughter at the crude jokes passed back and forth in the family effort to amuse her and make her feel at home. Often she "went from top to bottom" with a spring clean in the time she was with us, taking down the curtains in a genuine wish to help in the frantic rush of shop life, but often not knowing how.

Thankfully, life with Granny was calmer, and the morning after Mum and Dad had left us would find us awake early, especially if the sun was shining. In those August days it usually was, streaming in through the top of the sash window, and on to our faces as we awoke. Our few clothes, unpacked the night before, were hurriedly chosen and thrown on, cotton print dresses with bows tied by each other at the back, and T-bar sandals, straps fastened with fumbling fingers in the hurry to get down to the breakfast table. Granny's porridge with milk and a thick trail of treacle in a swirl to the middle was quickly put before us and the homemade bread and honey to follow stood in the centre of the kitchen table. Sometimes, it was one of Miss Taylor's freshly gathered eggs, soft boiled, the yolks bright orange and runny, and a plate of Granny's special soldiers spread with butter. The eggs were gleefully bashed about the top and the shell picked off and put on the side of the plate, to be sprinkled later on the bed of snapdragons in the garden to fertilise the soil. Nothing was ever wasted in Granny's house. We ate all our meals at the kitchen table. There was no sitting with a plate on our knee, it just wasn't done, and we all sat down in the small scullery, as she called it, for all our meals.

Our hair was a bit of a dilemma to Granny. She wasn't as adept at parting it and putting in the bows as Mum, so it was sometimes left without and fastened back at both sides with a bobby clip, the colourful ribbons left in the drawer. Not that we bothered; we were always in a hurry to get out to play, and the ribbons were a nuisance anyway, easily pulled off by the boys in their rough play. Granny "did" her housework in the mornings, clad in her oldest dress and wrap-around floral pinny, her snow-white hair pin-curled and covered with a fine invisible hairnet or, if the work involved batting any rugs, a scarf tied turban-style around her head as she batted and shook furiously at the rugs hung over the garden wall. The housework usually involved cleaning the range in the living room and raking out the ashes, which left a fine sediment of dust everywhere that she whisked away with a feather duster, from the top of the sideboard, the highly polished drop-leaf table, and the old gramophone, one of her proudest possessions.

She had lots of music too, from popular songs of the day right through to the big band music, orchestral marches, and polkas. She had a very wide taste and played the records constantly as she did her housework, pausing now and again to wind the handle as the music slowed down, speeding it on its way with a quick half dozen turns. We had our favourites and some records were bought by her especially for us. We almost wore out *Teddy Bears' Picnic*, and were encouraged to join in her rendition of the chorus of *Rose Marie*, one of her favourites, sung loudly and very out of tune as the feather duster was whisked around the room. The gramophone was our entertainment on wet days, and we often wore out the needle, having to replace it with a new one, kept in a hollow by the turntable. They were never thrown away so it was often a case of finding the best blunt one, the worst of them causing the arm to slip across the record and leave a scratch, causing a blip here and there as the arm jumped over to a fresh place. When the records weren't on, she listened to the wireless. *Music While You Work* and *Workers' Playtime* were the programmes of the day, and she often paused for a while to listen, sometimes waltzing around the room, arms up, holding an imaginary partner, housework forgotten, and pure pleasure on her face. She loved to dance, and Old Time especially, doing a Two Step around the room, whisking over the furniture in time to the music and swishing at the corner cobwebs in flourishes to fit the music beat. Many a wet afternoon saw us pushing the furniture back to learn the St Bernard's Waltz or the Valeta, taking turns to dance with her around the room. We always finished with a boisterous Gay Gordons before tea was got ready in the scullery after she had caught her breath. We would sit on the bottom three steps of the staircase protruding into the room, closed off from the rest of the stairs by a door, and our favourite place to sit when she was busy "doing". The back door was held on a chain, giving us a four-inch view of any clearing of the weather and a chance to play. We were never bored, she was perfect entertainment, often tiring herself out as she tried to keep up with our young legs. Then a quiet moment to catch herself up was called for, "resting her eyes" as she nodded in the fireside chair.

Housework done, dinner prepared, Granny would don her brown herringbone tweed coat and hat and round us up for shopping. Knees inspected and dusted down, we were gathered to her like chicks to begin the journey down Rose Avenue to New Road Side, where she picked up her daily requisites at the shops, the butcher's, the baker's, the greengrocer's, and the Co-op, stopping to chat occasionally and show off "Marion's twins". It was a ritual started at about eleven o'clock most days, when the morning's little jobs of necessity were done, leaving time to get home to cook the dinner in time for Auntie Phyllis whose daily visits coincided with her dinner hour. It was always a dinner, the main meal of the day, potatoes, vegetables, and meat of some sort. She had a very good diet, despite the rationing, and we also had a pudding with custard, a rare treat for us as Mum was always too busy to bother with one, leaving us to help ourselves out of the shop window most of the time. Granny's meals were simple and tasty, for she was a good cook, and if the meat ration was small, there was always some bread and butter served with it. The prompting that "Bread makes Bonny Bairns" in the effort to fill us up was uttered in unison around the table. It was one of Granny's peculiar sayings that we picked up and laughed about when we got home and back to the Shippam's Paste of Derby Street teatimes, when the large pile of bread on a plate and a variety of jars appeared on the table regularly.

Auntie Phyllis always brought her dog with her, picked up from home on her way to Granny's. Judy was a black Labrador, and flopped on the scullery coconut matting at our feet, waiting for titbits from all our plates. We watched for them coming down the street, shouting to Granny to dish out the dinner when they turned the corner and were in sight. Then we all sat down, Jean and I making the effort not to talk with our mouths full, which was frowned on by Granny at all times. Dinner once over, gossip discussed, Auntie Phyllis took Judy home and went back to work, while Granny washed up and sat down to "rest her eyes". Occasionally the room would reverberate with the sound of light snoring. Eyes rested, it was time for the "wash and change" at the scullery sink, which was

116

Granny's bathroom, and the preparations for the afternoon stroll when work clothes were changed for the walking-out clothes, to stroll through Horsforth Hall Park. We didn't escape either and were washed and changed, and the hair bows tackled, to stroll the meandering footpaths with her, calling at the pavilion café to partake of a Walls ice cream cornet while sitting on a bench watching people pass by, the main entertainment on such occasions.

Horsforth Hall Park was at one time someone's country pile. The house, now long demolished, must have been rather grand, with a walled garden, stables, bluebell wood, and lots of pleasant parkland leading to a raised bank where the house was once situated. There was a stone retaining wall beneath which there was a trickle of a moat of some kind, now turned into a dried-up ditch full of nettles and long grass over which a small bridge took the drive up a sweep of smooth lawn to where the house once stood. The lawn was landscaped with rhododendrons and tall pine trees and conifers, providing a pleasant area to sit on the ornamental benches, dotted here and there. There were tennis courts in a walled garden where Mum played tennis in her youth, and a bank of seating for spectators, rising up against the wall. Granny remembered the house before it was pulled down, and said it was very grand. Later years saw it in a sad state of repair, and it was deemed dangerous and pulled down. The stables were still there, or something was. I vaguely remember some buildings in a red brick at the back of the park where the park keeper hung about and chased us off when occasionally our play ventured near. We could still imagine the carriages in the previous century sweeping through the imposing gates and up the curving drive, all very grand, to the beautiful house, and stopping on the bank of daisy-dotted lawn, where we made the daisy chains under the giant fir trees, to deposit the gentry at the grand entrance to the Hall. Only the echo of its grandeur remained and the parkland was now given over to the hoi polloi.

The park was a large part of our childhood, and Mum and Dad's too, I dare say, as much of their courting was done there before the war. The stone wall surrounding it must have had railings at one time because the remnants of them jutted out about an inch or so, giving us an assault course to tiptoe through, trying to avoid the metal stumps that were left when they were cut off for the war effort. The wall with its broken teeth ran parallel with the road that swept through Horsforth and on past Auntie Phyllis's in Broadway Drive, and then on past Granny Toothill's back garden, and up to Auntie Vera's further along. It was just at the top of Granny's street and gave us a safe place to play, the traffic being virtually nil in those days as we hung about alternately sitting and tiptoeing along its length. Of all the parks of our childhood, it was our favourite, and made Bolton's parks look drab in comparison, having a grandeur sadly lacking in our town parks, and it was special in our young eyes as we played with our friends and took our strolls with Granny in our best dresses and on our best behaviour.

118

Then it was home for tea, fished from the depths of the cellar under the scullery, going down to its icy flag floor to take the bread from the cloth-covered earthenware bread urn, and choose the cake from the various cake tins stored on the stone ledge. Tea was usually bread and butter, with jam or honey, and cake, all homemade by Granny and laid on plates with a crisp white lacy doily on the scullery table. It was usually taken after she had listened to *Mrs. Dale's Diary* with her ear to the wireless, trying to hear above our din, often shooing us into the back yard so she could listen in peace. Once it was over we were called in for tea.

Then we were allowed to get changed and play out until bedtime with the rest of the kids in the street, most of whom were our age or thereabout. It was a happy little gang, and our games were similar to the ones we played in Bolton. Other games we played were country-based, like tracking in the country lanes, a version of hare and hounds using chalk arrows instead of paper. We made bogies too, out of old pram wheels and wooden crates and bits of string, pulling one another around in them, and racing each other down the steep street, crashing into a garden wall to stop them in the absence of brakes. Mum, when we got home, would despair at our shoes, the soles worn well away in a couple of weeks on a bogie. In hindsight, it was a dangerous occupation, having no way to stop them, only our feet, and a well-placed playmate to catch us at the bottom and turn us into the wall before we careered into the road. Luckily there was very little traffic, despite it being the main road into Leeds, but we never thought about the dangers; children never do. When we acquired roller skates, Granny realised the danger after a neighbour had seen us careering down the steep street and crashing into the wall to stop, going straight to Granny and ratting on us. She would only let us wear one skate after that, visualising a visit to hospital if we carried on.

We made dens in the long grass, flattening out a circle in the fields to play in, and trailed the country lane in a gang, spying on courting couples in barns. It was very different to Bolton's terraced streets, and was certainly cleaner and more informative. Sex was more open in Horsforth and the kids were very "aware". Bolton's kids were innocent compared to the Horsforth lot, who knew all the "cheeky" talk.

I think we heard the F-word there for the first time, but not knowing what it was it remained a mystery to us which is a good job because it wasn't used like it is now, and Mum would have been quite shocked. A lot of the talk was bravado with a lot of guessing involved, but still, it was a lot more open than in Bolton where sex was never mentioned. As we grew older, Granny let go a bit, allowing us to disappear with our playmates for hours on end, only coming back when we were hungry. No doubt this caused her endless worry, not knowing where we were. Usually we were trawling the country lanes or could be found in the Hall park, sprawling on the grass playing truth or dare. Our games were very varied but were non-mischievous to others. Vandalism was not in our nature, either, being rewarded with a thick ear for any damage we did, accidentally or on purpose.

Bus fares were cheap and a few coppers would get us to Rawdon Park, rather a dull place but it did have swings to while away an hour or so, and a sweet shop from which to buy a frozen Jubbly to suck on till it went white and all the flavour had gone. The swimming baths at Pudsey were another regular day out. Walking there with our costumes rolled up in a towel and vying for a space to swim in the crowded baths, we stood chest high, hugging the side in the effort to avoid being ducked by some bully of a boy egged on by his mates. It was almost impossible to swim because the baths were always so crowded. It was a constant battle of the sexes. We almost drowned in the process, and there were regular whistles blown and boys sent out in disgrace after a run from the diving board to jump in on top of us. We were almost glad when the hour was up, it was so rough. Despite the rough baths, we never swam in ponds and rivers, so on hot days we braved it with the rest. Occasionally Granny would take us and the better-behaved of our playmates to Yeadon Dam to fish for minnows with a net. It was only shallow, and if we did fall in we could stand up. It was very clean then, too, and we sat on the bank to eat our picnic. The minnows were brought home in a jam jar, tied round the top with a bit of string to make a handle. They always died, despite our care of them, probably from shock and lack of oxygen. They were buried in Granny's snapdragon patch, in a matchbox, with a little prayer and a cross made from matchsticks. It would have been better to put them back, but it wouldn't have been the same. Juggling with the jam jar on the bus added to the fun of the day out.

The days were usually long, sunny and hot, but we did have some holidays when it rained a lot, leaving us sitting on the bottom half of the twisty staircase, the three steps inside the scullery door, to peer out at the rain through the four-inch gap the door chain allowed. Any break in the clouds gave us hope and sent us racing up the street to call for Brenda and the rest of the Rose Avenue gang. Brenda was our best friend in Horsforth. She lived further up the street with her Mum and Dad, brother, and Grandma. When we were there in summer, they were usually getting ready to go to Butlin's at Filey for their summer holiday, so she was always excited, telling us about all the things to do at Butlin's. In those days I suppose it was exciting.

Horsforth was quite a rural place compared to Bolton. There were no mills and no slum streets, and only two picture houses, no brothel across the road to watch either, so I suppose you could say entertainment was limited. Granny's highlights of the day must have been her morning trip to the shops and the dressed-up afternoon stroll, especially after she had lost Grandad. The shopping was usually done on New Road Side; it wasn't often she went up Town Street where the main rows of shops were. She was partial to a sixpenny mix from the fish and chip shop in Back Lane, usually calling on her way home if she'd had call to go up Town Street. The shops on New Road Side were nearer for her, and she would walk down dressed in a brown herringbone tweed coat and felt hat, carrying her wicker shopping basket. She always wore a hat outside, putting it on in front of the mantel mirror, spearing it with a long hatpin and tidying any hair sticking out, before she went out. They were always of the felt variety in various designs, giving her the appearance of Miss Marple at times, especially the broad brimmed one which was rather battered at the edges.

Monday was the one day she missed, that being "washing day", when the leftovers from the Sunday joint were hashed in a pot to simmer while the washing was got out of the way and draped across the street to dry. This was always started early, with the dolly tub being brought up from the cellar and filled in stages from the gas geyser. The whites were put in first and pummelled well with the posser, which was an upside down basin with holes in to force the water through and a long handle. Well-possed to get out the dirt, the washing was hauled out, manually wrung by twisting, and rinsed in the sink. Then it was manually wrung again to lift out some of the water before being put through the big wooden mangle several times. The dirtier clothes were then washed, Granny often having to scrub them on the washboard, a narrow corrugated metal plate which stood in the dolly tub at an angle and was used in conjunction with a stiff scrubbing brush. It was very hard work, her face turning a bright red in the heat and the effort of the brisk scrubbing through several lots of washing. The lines were put out and the washing hung across the street with the neighbours' washing. On a brisk day the sight of it was spectacular, blowing in the wind, propped high to get as much air to it as possible. The coalman gave these back streets as wide a berth as possible on Mondays, the designated day for washing. Any brave creature trying to deliver was berated forcefully, the washing as fiercely guarded as a national treasure and inspected for finger marks at the sound of any lorry down the back street. Many a row was started at a request to lift up the lines to allow a vehicle through, the driver slinking away, tail between his legs, and having to return the next day. They took no prisoners; Monday was the day and that was that.

On shopping days, the first call was at the fruit and veg shop. A very plain place with a basic supply of vegetables of the old English sort — carrots, cauliflowers, cabbage, peas, potatoes. None of the exotic sort to be found in supermarkets today. All were stored in open wooden trays, or in boxes on legs, mostly unwashed and I suppose organic. The carrots came with green tops which was a regular sight in those days, the greengrocer cutting them off at Granny's request and wrapping them in newspaper after weighing them on a big scale with iron weights. There was no serving yourself either. You got what you were given, and that was that. The greengrocer, whose name I can't recall, wore a brown overall and cloth cap that matched the brown paper bags, threaded on a piece of string nailed to each box. The limit of his conversation was " 'morning" and a bit of local gossip acquired from earlier customers. Granny didn't dawdle here long. It was business done and on to the grocer's, Mr. Grindrod, whose shop was across the road. Very much like Mr. Pearson's, this little shop of high shelves containing all and sundry could involve a lengthy wait to be served. The daily ritual was played out with at least another six people in the queue, local gossip flying back and forth as one person replaced another in the line waiting for Mr. Grindrod's attention. Gradually inching nearer the front, Granny's turn eventually came and, once served and gossip taken in tow, the ritual was once more played out in Hinchcliffe's, the baker's next door. Further along and across the road Chadwick's, Hinchcliffe's main competition, was where Granny bought her potted meat and deposited the gossip taken in tow. This was a lengthier call, because Mrs. Chadwick was friendly with Grandma Toothill and always enquired after Mum and Dad, often passing on the news of Mum's in-laws to Granny along with the potted meat. We always hung about the shop front, counting the wasps in the window. We were terrified of wasps, giving us an excuse not to go into the shop in case we were "buzzed". I think Granny was relieved too, not to have us dancing around her coat tails when she was trying to acquire the news about the other side of the family and the potted meat before it "went off". Chadwick's was opposite the Glenroyal, the local picture house, so we would go to look at the posters, pestering Granny to go and see the film if it was one we fancied. Promises given, we would all go after tea, sitting in the stalls, one either side of her, so we could share the mint imperials, "chapel mints" to us. Granny was very partial to them, with a six penn'orth always in

125

her handbag to suck discreetly from the crumpled bag at moments of opportunity and in church.

Our next port of call was the Co-op, an early version of a supermarket, which we found fascinating as we were able to play with the swing barriers going in and out. It was very small by today's standards and wasn't all that well stocked. Sugar was weighed out and put into blue sugar bags and butter cut from a big block, patted into a small oblong shape with butter patters. Always fascinating to watch was the bacon counter, displaying the sides of bacon and the bacon slicing machine. Granny would pick the bacon, the leanest she could find and well-smoked, and have it cut "thin, please, just two slices". The biscuits were in big tins all in a line with clear glass lids that lifted up, sports biscuits, malted milk, Nice, and several chocolate ones that were called chocolate variety, all mixed up and white where they were scuffed. She let us put a few in a bag occasionally, and rationed them to make them last, otherwise they would all have been eaten in one sitting. The shopping was then all put into the basket and paid for at the barrier, with her Co-op number and Co-op "divi" being entered at the same time. A brown shiny carrier bag with string handles could be bought, but Granny always had her wicker basket because you had to pay for those. Even so, they were very sturdy and have recently made a comeback in posh shops after all these years. Next door to the Co-op was that other British institution, the Co-op Butchers, a white-tiled mausoleum of hanging dead animals with a carpet of sawdust on the floor to soak up the blood. It was here

Granny bought her weekend joint and the other cheaper cuts of meat we ate through the week, while we piled up the sawdust with our feet into little piles as we waited in the queue. Huge carcases hung around the walls on hooks from the ceiling rail, the small drips of blood coagulated in the sawdust on the tiled floor. It was all gruesome, including the poor chickens with heads and feathers, their poor wrung necks at an angle as they dangled by their feet in the window. All the trays were running with blood too; it was certainly not the pristine plastic sterile trays of meat we see today. There was a striped curtain hung in the the doorway to keep out the flies and bluebottles buzzing about excitedly in the vicinity, but it didn't keep in the smell distinctive to butchers, of blood and sawdust. We would have been glad to wait outside, but then the sawdust drew us in, it was too good to resist.

After the morning shopping was done, we would call at Miss Taylor's in Rose Terrace, the next street to Rose Avenue. Granny bought her eggs and tomatoes from Miss Taylor, who was an old lady like Granny. She was a great character, with a big garden at the back of her house, in which she grew a variety of vegetables in summer. They were laid out in rows. Cabbages and lettuce, spring onions, carrots, leeks, all lined up and shipshape from the path, with a flattened furrow between each of the rows where feet had trampled to pick the harvest. It was a cottage garden too, with marigolds and sweet peas nodding alongside the garden peas. The banks of dahlias and tall chrysanthemums added colour here and there before they were picked and sold for a few coppers to all who admired them, with the produce grown in abundance over the summer.

Miss Taylor kept hens too, along with a colony of cats, all roaming at will in the large garden. Jean and I were often sent to hunt for eggs between the rows of vegetables when we called, while Granny talked to Miss Taylor about Chapel goings on. The cats and hens lived in harmony, both in and out of the house through which they seemed to wander regardless of the many shooings to keep them under control. There were lots of kittens too, tumbling over the fireside chair in which Miss Taylor sat, and through the knitting basket she always seemed to be sorting through. Granny often took her bits of wool, left over from our cardigans, for which she was grateful. Her house was open to anyone who called and, despite the mess made by cats and hens alike, it was homely. We were always warmly welcomed, and taken through to the garden to seek out the eggs and to play with the kittens on the rug in the small back room. We were sent to pick peas too, and to choose a lettuce which was cut from the soil with a knife and wrapped in newspaper for us to carry home.

After we had been to Miss Taylor's, it was home in time for Granny to put the potatoes and vegetables on top of the gas stove and switch on the oven to cook the pudding and meat. We would lay the table and help make the custard, standing on a stool with Granny holding us around the middle to make sure we didn't fall off or get burned while we took turns to stir. Such were our days at Granny's, long and full of pleasures, with good memories to take into our future. The days passed quickly by though, and in no time at all Mum and Dad turned up to take us home again, the two weeks in the country having flown by. Granny was kissed goodbye, and a quiet tear shed in the back seat of the car as it climbed over Blackstone Edge and back to Lancashire and life without her.

CHAPTER
SEVEN

Bolton in the Fifties

Much as we loved Horsforth, our life really was in Bolton. We were turning into Lancashire Lasses with our "Lanky" twang. As we moved up through the juniors at school, we developed friendships with other girls in our class. Friends made at five were to be our friends into adolescence to when we left school at sixteen, each to go our own way in life in the wide and often confusing world. We all went through the infants and juniors together, took our scholarships, and eventually all ended up at the same school, Hayward School, a large base containing three schools, grammar, technical and secondary, a new idea at the time. When I passed a scholarship and Jean didn't, it allowed us to remain together to a certain extent, and to meet up at dinnertime for the journey home. It was the first time we had been separated.

Jean and several of our friends were still together in the same class. I was put separately in the technical school, which was a bit daunting as I didn't know anyone. But I soon made friends, so we had two separate sets of friends from then onwards. The teachers were somewhat confused for a time as we seemed to be in two places at once, and we were nailed once or twice for being in the "wrong place" and out of bounds. Eventually the situation evened out when it was sussed there were two of us, even if they couldn't tell who was who. Pamela, Sandra and Julie remained with Jean until the final year at school, when streaming put us all in the same class, so we all finished as well as started school together, on the same day. Our friendships were sometimes volatile, but we all remained good friends until we all slowly drifted apart when we acquired steady boyfriends and eventually married.

After school and during the holidays, we all met to go swimming at the High Street Baths or to The Nevada, our local roller-skating rink, spending our afternoons together chatting and laughing and watching the boys. The Nevada was a popular place, better than the rink over Bridgeman Street Baths where we had learned to skate as youngsters, holding on to the rail around the room in the effort to stay on our feet. It played pop music, too, and had a bar and café where we could sit and watch when we weren't skating. The only disadvantage was that, being so crowded as the session went on, the smell of under-arm sweat pervaded the place. Dad always called it "Heinz varieties", we always called it "soup". Deodorants weren't widely used in the 1950s, and washing was needed every day to keep the smell at bay. It was a common problem, especially in summer when it was hot. Mum and Dad sometimes came with us in the evenings and we had loads of fun, linking arms and skating in a row. We couldn't do the dances, although Mum and Dad often had a bash at the skaters' waltz, not very elegantly, I might add, and getting in every one's way because there wasn't the room. We found it almost impossible to skate backwards and never did manage to learn, despite Dad's tuition, giving up after a few bad falls. We never quite managed to keep the momentum going.

The High Street Baths was our local swimming pool where we went regularly. It was somewhat rough by today's standards and was overrun with cockroaches at times. They floated on the water here and there and had to be fished out with a net on a long handle by the pool attendant, who was the lifeguard, the cleaner, and one-man band. He controlled the place, blowing the whistle at bad behaviour and calling the band colours to come out when we'd had our money's worth. When it was busy, which it nearly always was after school and in the school holidays, that was after one hour. We could have stayed in all afternoon, watching our fingers wrinkle up, and it was warm in summer because the sun shone on the water and warmed it. But we were always rounded up and thrown out to let more people in. Cockroaches or not, it was cheap, and the cockroaches were an added attraction, lifting them out as we made a futile attempt to learn the breaststroke. It wasn't very nice though to stand on one in the changing cubicles around the pool; they made a loud crack, and that sickening feeling as you lifted your foot up and peeled them off the bottom of your foot was horrible. Some of the boys hunted them down, counting the score of who stamped on most. Horrible, but typical of boys.

The boys changed on the balcony above the pool with very little privacy, but we girls had cubicles, with a louvered door that just about covered the middle bits. Anyone in the pool could see your legs up to your knees and a bit above, so it became a habit of the regular cheeky boys to hug the side of the pool, looking up to see what they could spy. With the doors being louvered and the walkway only narrow, that was quite a bit, so some smirks and nudges ensued in little groups until the pool attendant caught on and blew the whistle to break them up. After the spell in the pool, despite it being warmed by the sun, we were always freezing and shivering when we got dressed. All wrinkled up after an hour in the pool, hair wet despite the bathing caps we were forced to wear, it was time to adjourn to "Manfredi's" to thaw out, each hugging a glass of hot Vimto or sarsaparilla, guaranteed to warm us up and set our teeth on edge. We would sit around their glass and wrought iron tables until we got noisy and were thrown out for not buying another glass. Still, by that time our hair had dried for the walk home down Derby Street.

Dad had acquired a car by then, so Sundays would find us with flask and picnic piling into the car with fingers crossed, hoping it would start, for a day out on Mum and Dad's only day off. It was an old Morris Twelve, in black, with a running board he would let us ride on up the back street. Very smart, but rather ancient compared to Billy Pike's slick Vanguard. Dad

POOH STICKS IN THE GUTTER

joined him to proudly polish it in the back street while preparations for the day out were in process, Mum calling a halt to the proceedings when she appeared with the flask in the effort to jog the preparations along, finally losing patience with a "Well, are we going or not?" as Dad and Billy sought to outshine and out-talk one another as they polished. Dad used it for deliveries through the week, but Sundays when we eventually got going were for fun. It wasn't much fun for the poor AA man as the day out was a bit hit and miss at times. It would often break down and the petrol gauge had a bad habit of sticking, but the AA man always got us home, patching us up on the side of the road after Dad had hitched a lift to the nearest call box. Often the mere lifting of the bonnet inveigled some kind Samaritan to pull up and tinker at the plugs and carburettor along with Dad. The car would sit chugging and choking at the side of the road, and backfiring as if to protest, sending Mum into panic at the thought of spending the night there or having to catch the bus home. Nothing daunted Dad, and, tinkering and pacifying at the same time having failed, he regularly set off to walk, thumb in the air with one of us in tow, to get help. He certainly had his money's worth from the AA; we must have been notorious because they all recognised us, and saluted us despite it all. But then again it might have been because of the AA badge Dad brightly polished before we set off, just on the off chance.

How times have changed. In those days it was common to be helped at the side of the road. Many a motorist would help another who had broken down.

Dad often did, giving a lift to the nearest call box when he couldn't help any other way, the poor motorist sitting between us in the back seat. A lot of our days out were to Morecambe and Arnside, where Dad would fish for flatties after digging his bait on the sands before the tide came in, often beating a quick retreat as the water swept in encircling us. Once Dad got stuck in the quicksand, his wellies sucked down six inches while Jean and I panicked on the edge of the dig. He sat down and calmly pulled his feet out of them, then managed to make his way to us to calm us down and pull the wellies out of the sucking mud. The sands were very precarious and after that we were extra careful, not going too far out with Mum keeping a watchful eye from the shore. He dug great holes in the silty sand, while we kept our eyes open for juicy lugworms and swooped down to put them in the bucket, ever keeping a wary eye on the incoming tide. The water always came in very fast, and five minutes lingering too long for that extra dig could get you cut off. More than once we had to wade back knee deep in water when the tide swept in behind us, leaving us on a sand bank, after our attention was taken by the search for the elusive "King Rag", the best bait. We had some lovely days there over the years, and Mum would fry up the flatties for supper when we got home.

Eventually, in later years, Mum and Dad bought a caravan there and went on Saturday afternoons when they had shut the shop. Saturday nights, we went into Morecambe and walked the prom, calling at Hest Bank for a bag of chips on the way back, eating them

135

watching the sunset over the bay until the windows steamed up. Parked on the bumpy grass verge among the pools over the railway line, we were thoroughly deafened when a train went past at full speed. It was the main line up to Scotland and they were frequent in those days, and on time.

Life must have been very dull before Dad's car for afterwards our lives revolved around it. Nice as it was to be mobile, it could also be a pain in the neck, and the cause of the many fracas with Billy Pike in the back street. One weekend Dad decided it was in dire need of a re-spray. Egged on by his tinkering mate Reg, they rigged up a home-made "spray gun", and attached it to Mum's vacuum cleaner hose. The idea was that the sucking hose when reversed would blow the paint on to the car in a fine spray. Unfortunately the theory didn't come up to scratch, and the effect was a blotchy mess, with blobs of paint splattered here and there. Some parts were better than others. The best was like orange peel, but a few runs marred the shiny bits, and Dad, non-plussed and looking on the bright side so to speak, decided the finish would be O.K. when polished with rubbing paste, guiltily produced by Reg, to even it out and bring up the shine. After two long days of rubbing with bits of cotton waste from the mill and the evil smelling rubbing paste, all we achieved was sore fingers, blisters, and odd bits of high sheen, while the rest of the damned thing remained pretty much the same. Damage done, that's how it stayed, but the extra layers of paint did deter the rust a bit, so maybe it was worth all the hard work. Nobody held it against Reg, although he managed to stay out of the way a while, and in time his mastery of mechanics was called for again and often.

Eventually, after Reg or Alf Martin from the Britannia Garage became a permanent presence in the back street, the Morris Twelve was declared redundant, its boxy shape old-fashioned and dated, which Billy Pike had pointed out all along, much to Dad's distain. Now he was right and it was Dad's excuse to put his nose out of joint when a sleek black and white Zephyr with flashy red seats appeared, in which we all rode about like royalty. Dad positively purred, polishing with Billy in the back street. And for a time, Billy would slink in, tail between his legs, leaving Dad to polish alone, triumphant in the one-upmanship stakes. After a while the novelty wore off, and it was deemed "tinny and rather flash", with Dad hankering for a Simca from afar. Mum was eventually talked round and gave in. The flashy Zephyr disappeared when it was paid for and a new hire purchase appeared. French and chic to look at, it was Dad's pride and joy for a while, even if it did sound like an old sewing machine. As all things French were, it was flighty and very naughty at times, with the spare parts costing a fortune. Dad soon fell out of love with the continental floosy and when the H.P. was up his eyes lighted upon a metallic blue Sunbeam Talbot. It was a beauty and even Mum was impressed, despite the spiralling H.P. Dad kept that for some time, probably to pay off the extra H.P. and in the meantime Billy bought a new Vanguard. Same boring old thing.

But Billy was classic and of the old guard, so they were "Even Steven" for a while.

Dad like most men measured his financial status by his cars, and, while none of them were brand new, he managed to spend a fortune much to Mum's dismay. Covering the H.P. debt came out of the housekeeping budget, but it was Dad's only pleasure, ours too on Sundays. There was a succession of newish cars over the years, Dad excited as ever about each one until he really put Billy's nose out of joint with a brand new one in the mid-1960s, a Vauxhall 2000 in bottle green metallic. He gave up tinkering in the back street then as all subsequent cars were under warranty, and he had no further excuse to "meddle", much to Mum's relief and the relief of Mr. Pike, who could once more get into his garage.

Saturday afternoons in winter usually meant a trip to Manchester, especially if we were due new clothes. Mum was an avid shopper when we had the money. It was usually in spurts, depending on the state of her finances and the seasons. We were apt to grow rapidly out of our things, despite the six-inch hems which left a line of ingrained dirt and wear showing when let down, and we were bought at least one new outfit at Easter and for winter every year, for "best". Rather a snazzy dresser in her youth, Mum preferred the shops in Manchester town centre, which were on the whole more fashion-conscious and had more variety. Some were chain stores which were cheaper for us, namely C&A, and Lewis's. When she wanted to be posh, we looked round Kendall's and Marshall and Snelgrove's

138

with her tutting quietly at the prices on the price tags before we were dragged over to C&A for something "more sensible". It was always a toss up between Lewis's and C&A, and we were to-ing and fro-ing between the two to compare things and try on before we bought. There was a big Marks and Spencer's too, with racks of things you couldn't try on, making it a bit difficult at times when we were growing so fast. It was all mahogany then, with high counters we couldn't see over and bare wooden floorboards, not the sleek place it is today. Mum always bought our underwear there, knickers, vests and liberty bodices; you couldn't beat it for price or quality.

Mum bought her corsets there, or girdle, to hold her stomach in. Dad called it a roll-on, because that's how she got it on, tugging and rolling it up over her stomach. It wasn't much good either, and she took it off at night to sit comfortably, rolling it down and stepping out of it smartly with a sigh of relief, especially when it was new and still had the elastic intact. After a while it became slack and yellowed with all the washing, but it bedded in and she didn't have to take it off at night for a bit of relief. The suspenders that dangled from it were always popping off, and we all had to look for the little rubber buttons off them in the house. If they popped off outside, it was too embarrassing to look, so she would wear a sixpence slotted where the little buttons should be, holding up her stockings.

When we were sixteen she bought us one each, but we were too thin for it to make any difference. She said it would give us "support" and stop our bottoms sagging. The fashion was for full skirts with tiny wasp waists and blouses with Peter Pan collars. We wore twin sets, too, just like Mum, mini-versions of course. There were no teenage fashions then and children's fashions were in the same style as adults. C&A were a little more flexible and it was cheap and cheerful, Mum's favourite store and Dad's everlasting chore. He hated shopping and would hang about outside the changing rooms as we tried on one thing after another. He was always there though when we popped out for his opinion, looking blank and nodding at everything as Mum pulled and fluffed out the outfits we tried on. Despite having to be dressed alike, we were allowed to choose the colour occasionally, and any difference of opinion was settled by Mum in the end, sulks breaking out on the way home in the back of the car. If this happened, there was always a threat to take the outfits back and the ultimate threat of banishment to a children's home, causing us to clam up and be glad of what we got, and think what lucky girls we were. Despite the threats, she still sewed for us in the afternoons when the shop was slack, making summer dresses out of cotton for little cost.

Once the major business of outfit buying was over, Dad got his turn. I think he only came for Lewis's Food Hall, and that was where we always ended up. He visibly lightened as we approached on the down escalator, diving off, making a beeline for the pie and cake counters, standing drinking it all in, making mental notes and comparing their prices with his own.

New lines were compared, sized and inspected. Some were bought, and any samples tasted with glee, deep in thought as he pondered. Mum would rebuke him with a sharp "Come on, Cyril, haven't you seen enough of that all week?" and drag him protesting away. He would always buy a pork pie to relish and dissect for tea, prodding at the meat content and aspic jelly with his knife before he tasted it, and pass comment to Mum over the table at tea.

In winter the journey home was often horrific, when the pea-souper fog came down. Once it took us an hour and a half to get home. The fog was so thick Dad had to drive with his head out of the window to see where he was going. Mum had to keep the window down to judge how far we were off the curb, as the fog swirled round, damp and tasting of smoke, into the car. The fogs were very bad in November and they dirtied our faces, leaving smuts on all our clothes too.

Bolton was very different in the 1950s to today's Bolton. For one thing, the traffic was practically non-existent compared to today. The trolley buses that trawled regularly up and down Derby Street slowly disappeared, their place being taken by maroon double-deckers which chugged into gear from each bus stop, situated every three blocks. Following the slum clearances, when Dad faced a shortage of regular customers as whole streets were moved into the new housing estates in Great Lever and Breightmet and the flat desolation left was camped on by gypsies, we were often pestered to buy lucky heather and clothes pegs. Mum didn't like to turn them away in case they put a curse on her, so she often had her fortune told. After crossing their palm with as little silver as she could get away with, they always told her she was coming into money. A likely story, but Dad had his hopes raised when the land across the road was earmarked for a college of further education, hopefully leading to an increase in turnover when it was finally opened.

It was about this time he started catering for the army who had a territorial barracks in the town. Luckily it was just around the corner, in Fletcher Street. Every month or so they held a dance, a lively occasion to say the least, and Dad was called on to cater, providing a supper which Mum always called a running buffet. It certainly was to us. We spent a good deal of the time running up the stairs to the supper room with trays of this and that, brought in from the car in several journeys from the bakehouse in the back street. Despite all the hard work, it was good fun and a chance to stay up late as the evening didn't finish until well after midnight. By that time we were all truly tired out as the preparations started early, Dad making the pies and pasties when he had finished his other stuff for the shop. There were usually sandwiches to make too, which Mum made in the shop just before we set off. There was always a variety of small fancy cakes and pastries, all set out in wooden trays ready to be taken round earlier in the day and locked in the supper room away from any sneaking fingers. The supper room was well away from the bar, which was off the drill hall, and the band was on the dais at one end, so we could watch the goings on from the balcony set out with tables at the other end.

We loved these occasions, for which Mrs. Farr and Graham were enlisted to help as well, all dressed up with posh pinnies to help put the buffet out onto plates and serve. Dad or Mrs Farr would man the tea urn, filling the cups and saucers as requested, with Mum taking the money at the head of the queue, the till from the shop being taken to ring up the prices. When the M.C. announced "Supper is served, ladies and gentlemen," chaos broke out as the hungry dancers surged up the stairs to be first in the queue. The dances were very popular, so an hour of siege ensued as we endeavoured to serve them all quickly, and dish out the teas.

Most popular were Dad's meat pies, with grabbing hands diving through the queue. They nearly always came back for more and, no matter how many he made, the table was soon swept clean, leaving the late comers settling for the hot meat and potato and a scoop full of mushy peas. It wasn't a posh buffet, as it would be today, there were no dainty little salads, but it was good substantial fare, typical of a "Reet good Lancashire night out". It was us kids' job to collect the empty plates and the cups and saucers that were tucked away in any corners, to be taken back to the kitchen to be washed up when the queue had diminished. We all helped as the kitchen had to be left as we found it, stacking away the cups and saucers and plates in huge piles where we had found them. Once the dancing resumed, most people drifted away, but we always

143

manned the supper table to sell off anything that was left to the few who drifted up the stairs later.

When most of the work was done, we went to watch the dancing. There were always couples snogging in dark corners, so we watched them as well, hanging about on the balcony near the supper room. There was a piano in one of the little dark rooms, so that often proved a bigger draw than the snoggers, banging out tuneless notes at random until we were heard and the lid firmly closed and locked. We always enjoyed the night, despite the hard work, and Graham enjoyed it too. Later Mum and Dad would have a dance, and we all joined in when the spot prize dances were announced, hoping to win a box of chocolates in a posh box with a ribbon on. We did once, and Dad won a bottle of whiskey, which he swapped for chocolates with someone else.

Dad was also called on to cater for Remembrance Sunday, a big day at the barracks, when they all marched down to town with the military brass band to lay wreaths on the cenotaph steps. As it was November, a buffet of hot pies was laid out. Quite plain as suited the occasion. We weren't called on to serve, it was just a case of supplying the pies. No mushy peas either. A very sombre occasion. Sometimes we would follow them down after delivering the pies, all the troops smart in their best uniforms, remembering their dead colleagues, Dad too. It always reminded us of Empire Day, the twenty fourth of May, when we marched around the school yard carrying a Union Jack, standing to attention and singing the National Anthem. I don't suppose anyone knows when Empire Day is now, never mind celebrates it.

There was another big occasion in Bolton that has since died out, and that was the Catholic Walks. The whole of Bolton turned out to see that. The Catholic Churches of Bolton carried their statues of Christ around the town with a long procession behind. The children were all dressed the same, walking behind the statues, parents and grandparents following. It was lovely to watch, especially the queen and her attendants. Being chosen was a great honour, and big churches had long processions. St Peter and St Paul's was always a long one and we knew several of the walkers. The walks lasted most of the afternoon, winding in a big column around Bolton's town centre streets, stopping here and there to even out the column, it was so long. Our Fletcher Street Methodists had "sermons" when we walked around the streets, stopping here and there to sing a hymn or speak a prayer. When we were Brownies, we had to go walking in line in our Brownie dresses behind Brown Owl and Tawny Owl. Mum bought us new shoes, shiny patent leather with ankle straps that we weren't allowed to wear till the day, and new cotton socks in dazzling white as opposed to the usual grey they turned into with Bolton grime. The day was very long, made longer by the new shoes which rubbed big blisters on our heels, while the dazzling socks slipped neatly under our heels. Mum was very sympathetic, with a supply of unlimited plasters and Germolene from Mr Costello's, but made sure the next year, when we were dressed as singers in white dresses and shawls, that our shoes were well broken-in. The dresses were hopelessly impractical for Bolton, and were made by Mum. We played May Queen in them afterwards; after that they were worn once or twice on Sundays at Granny's. Usually in our May Queen games, we dressed up in one of Mum's skirts and borrowed her net curtains for the veil and train. It was a popular game after the Catholic Walks, and fisticuffs or whose Mum's dress it was often decided who was Queen, the victor proudly parading up the back street with her retinue of attendants, dress and train held aloft out of the dirt to avoid a rollicking from Mum.

We had a visit from the real Queen and Prince Philip one year. We were all walked down to Bradshawgate with our Union Jacks to be lined up to cheer. Being tall I was put at the back of the crowd, so all I got was a glimpse of a glass-topped car flashing past. Despite creeping forward a time or two, I was sussed and dragged back, and when they went past I waved my flag like all the rest in the wall of noise that greeted them. It seemed very disappointing after the long walk down Derby Street, and after another long walk back we were all sat down to draw the "picture". I drew a flag and a few heads, which is all I saw really. The teacher wasn't impressed, and I was made to do it again "properly".

Bolton's special day in the 1950s was when they played in the Cup Final. Although they didn't win, a massive crowd thronged the Town Hall Square to welcome them back. We were taken down to see them by Auntie Olive who worked for Dad. They rode through Bolton in an open-topped bus to the Town Hall civic reception, crowds of people following behind in a great surge. Somehow we all got separated in the crush. It was very frightening, especially for Auntie Olive trying to find us all. Eventually, young and frightened as I was, I managed to find my way home, the others all together just before me. It was awful for Auntie Olive trying to explain my absence, and I was greeted by a worried Mum and Auntie Olive who were just about to set off to look for me. No harm was done, and I suppose I would have been taken to the police station, as all lost children were, and Mum would have found me there in time. But it was a scary experience, a kind lady having helped me find my way home after seeing me in tears, taking me to the bottom of Great Moor Street and out of the crush.

Auntie Olive worked for Dad for quite some time, often taking us home with her to play with her daughter, another Jean, when she finished work. In the holidays Jean played in the back street with us and Graham, leading the skirmishes down to Carey Street. Granny Powell was her Granny and she didn't see her as one of the witches like we did. Even so we never went into that house with her. It smelled of snuff, and had flagged floors, covered with a rag rug. She sent her on errands, calling her away from us, and she had to go. Jean was obsessed with film stars, especially Jane Powell, who she wanted to be like when she grew up. She spent hours tap-dancing on the mill coal hole ledge where the mill shutters came down, twirling around, arms in the air, as we sat mesmerised, watching the show. Sometimes we joined in, and we must have been a source of amusement at times to the mill workers in the mill canteen, sniggering at the windows. Auntie Olive's house was where we first saw television, sitting cross-legged on the floor to watch Muffin the Mule and Whirligig. It was one of the early television sets, so small it had to have a magnifying screen in front of it. It took ages to warm up before the picture came on and cleared, then it was poor and crackly, with frequent intervals where they showed the potter's wheel and the test card while it buzzed. Even so we sat watching, eyes glued to the screen in amazement. We wanted one! When Jean's Dad and her big brother Young Jim came home from work, we were packed off home or out to play so they could have their tea. They lived in the back kitchen. They had a parlour but it was rarely used. We weren't allowed in, but it wasn't posh. The stone steps were donkey-stoned and led into the yard which was shared with another house and the Sweet Green Tavern. Auntie Olive was proud of the steps, and regularly donkey-stoned them. Jean told us to walk in the middle; they didn't like footprints on them, even in the back yard. The front entrance was never used because it meant walking through the parlour.

The yard was a wonderful place to play, because it had the pub barrels stored there, and an out-house in which to hide, and there were three outside toilets with plank and latch doors, just like Granny's. Outside, Trinity Street Infant School was just across the back spare land, with a stone flag upright wall that had good footholds in so you could look over and into the yard.

That was one of our main occupations hanging around there, climbing over and back again before the caretaker spotted us and chased us off. Then we would dare one another to go down the old air raid shelter into the dark, and count how long we could stay down. It was blocked off part way down and smelled of wee, no doubt from the old men who used it as a toilet on their way home from the pub. At the top there was a good rail to swing tipple-ups on. Eventually it was all filled in and the school knocked down for a new road. It's a car park now, but the Sweet Green Tavern still stands as an island between the main dual carriageway and a slip road, as well as the yard and Auntie Olive's. I was married at the church across the road: that still stands too. Jean and Auntie Olive went to live in one of the new council houses, up Breightmet and we lost touch, but I don't think she became a film star, despite all the practice on the coal hole ledge.

Mum used to take us to the doctor's nearby to join the queue to see him when we were ill. It was up some steps at the top of a dark building, where he had two rooms. There was no receptionist in those days. We used to have to queue, often from the top landing, taking a seat when they became available and watching for our turn. Often it was a two or more hour wait, leading to the more impatient people making a quick dash into the consulting room, out of turn and jumping the queue. We once waited four hours and felt tempted to do the same, but there was always someone waiting for those that did when they came out. We could hear the fracas through the thin walls on the landing. It was

149

a poor state of affairs, and led to lots of complaints. The doctor took a partner soon after, but it was still a long wait. They moved premises as well and had a receptionist, who turned the regular malingers away, and greeted the rest with a "You'll 'ave to wait," as she opened the door to a waiting room packed to the ceiling. I won't say she was a dragon, but she breathed fire and ran the place with an iron fist. It was a miracle when appointments were introduced, but the wait wasn't any less. Only was the sympathy. It's a good job we were all fit because we would have died waiting to see a "specialist", and the £5 fee to put you to the front of the queue would have been wasted. It was no small sum then, and when you were ill it was pay up or die. We think we are hard done by now, but back then it was dire. No wonder Mum dosed us daily. We went through Scott's Emulsion and Virol like no tomorrow, and had Fenning's Fever Cures and Little Lung Healers thrust down our throats at the first sneeze. The fire in our bedroom was stoked up to sweat it out of us, and it did. Mum hadn't time to wait in the doctor's, and if we were really poorly he was sent for. We listened, dreading his arrival at the bottom of the stairs with Mum reeling off our symptoms on the way up, dreading the cold thermometer and stethoscope, and the thoughtful "mmm". Luckily, apart from Jean's Scarlet Fever, the most we ailed were the usual childhood illnesses and coughs and colds. Once when Granny came to see us she had shingles, so Mum had to get him for her. There wasn't much he could do, and Mum plastered her with calamine, a regular remedy in those days to cool anything down, especially sunburn when our unprotected backs got caught. Dad laughed at the lengths she went to to keep us all fit, calling her a quack, quacking up the passage like a duck on his way to the bakehouse, as she dosed us all with bottles of this and that kept on the window sill so she wouldn't forget. Sometimes it outstripped the food supply, but it kept Mr. Costello and Dr. Ryan's open.

CHAPTER
EIGHT

Special Days

Christmas and Easter were no holidays for Mum and Dad. They meant a lot of extra work and late nights, when Dad worked well into the early hours in the run-up to the holiday. We were recruited too, to help out where we could. Christmas started weeks before as Dad made his Christmas cakes and put them away to mature, often using our bedrooms as extra storage with covered trays stacked up in various corners out of the way. Made in big slabs, they were easier to store, and they could be cut into size to order. He made round ones as well, in three sizes, the smallest suitable for the poor unfortunates left to spend Christmas on their own. They were always about three inches deep, and very moist and dark, with lots of dried fruit and peel, and whole glacé cherries rolled in flour to stop them sinking to the bottom of the cake. As Christmas approached, he would top them with golden marzipan, and royal icing, spiking it up to make a snow scene. We were called on to place the Santas, snowmen and robins, sticking them on with a blob of royal icing to stop them falling over. When the icing was set, Mum wrapped frills around them and put them in the glass display counter for people to choose one. Their name was then put on, with a small deposit of course. As they disappeared, we knew that Christmas was getting closer, a fact made clearer when the mince pies started to appear. Dad made dozens of mince pies. By the time Christmas arrived, we could barely stand the sight or smell of them. Like the Christmas cakes, they were stacked in our rooms so we couldn't get away from them, their pungent smell pervading every corner despite being well covered with a wooden tray.

Starting when we finished school, Dad paid us to help, topping up our spending money for the holidays and Bolton's New Year fair. Dad blocked the cases while we spooned in the mincemeat, then he rolled out the pastry in a swathe on the bakehouse table, leaving us to cut out the lids with a crimping cutter, heaping them into a floured pile. Then we dipped them in a saucer of water and stuck them on, tray after tray, or so it seemed, putting them to bake in the big oven in large batches. When they were cool, we took them out of the tins, placing them into the wooden trays, covered and taken upstairs to be stacked in huge piles wherever there was a space. The week leading up to Christmas was hectic, and we all worked well into the night. Despite the hard work, it was a lovely atmosphere, with all of us excited as Christmas crept nearer.

Dad made lots of fancy little cakes specially for Christmas; fondant and chocolate covered, rich with butter cream and sugary and chocolate strands, rich rum truffles and chocolate cups, and meringues dipped in chocolate and sandwiched with whipped cream.

There must have been twenty different kinds, each in little paper cases, lined up in rows, decorated with silver balls and crunchy violet sugar petals. Mum made sherry trifles in waxed cartons onto which Dad piped fresh cream. We were allowed to drop on a bright red cherry and a pinch of chocolate strands, making sure the cherry was proud and in the middle above the cream. You could get tipsy with Mum's trifles; she always made sure that the sherry well and truly went in, there was no just showing them the bottle.

Dad excelled with the whist pies too, filling them to the very top with meat. He hated pork pies that were skimped on and kept the aspic to a minimum as he checked on the shrinkage in the oven, by cutting them in half, prodding at the meat, and popping them into his mouth to check the flavour. They must have met with approval, because people ordered them in droves along with his sausage rolls, puffy and fat from the oven. The night before Christmas saw him working all night to fill the extra orders of bread. It had to be fresh because it was unwrapped, and it was made at the last possible minute to last over Christmas.

The week before Christmas there were always lots of parties, for churches and schools. And the mill workers had their "footings", so called because of the old tradition of the bosses footing the bill as their thanks for their employee's hard work during the year. Unfortunately, that often turned out to be pasties all round, or a sausage roll, whist pie and a trifle each, eaten in the room where they worked. Even so, with most mill workers' sense of humour it would no doubt have proved most enjoyable, with the addition of a bit of mistletoe, and a drink or two to add to the merriment as the lasses "got at" the lads, with all the usual restriction removed.

By the time Christmas arrived, Mum and Dad were shattered. It's a good job Granny was there to help out. I don't know what they would have done without her. She both laughed and sympathised as they spent all Christmas Day asleep in front of the fire, and quietened our noise down occasionally when we got too excited playing the games out of our Christmas pillow case. Christmas Eve was chaos. The shop had orders stacked in every conceivable space, even in the house. We were sent on reconnaissance trips upstairs to track down any missing items, which wasn't easy as all the orders were now in white bags and white boxes, with various names on. As the goods were picked up, some boxes disappeared in the chaos, and Mum was constantly robbing Peter to pay Paul out of other people's orders, invariably being left short in the process. Then she would give them something out of ours, so often after all the hard work we stood and watched our Christmas goodies go out of the door. It's a good job we had the samples and rejects to try beforehand. The order book was dragged out too, as people forgot what they ordered, arguing in the shop and causing a blockage in the queue. Some had already paid for stuff, so that had to be checked, causing a bit of upset when Mum tried to charge them twice in the chaos. Desperation set in by five o'clock when there were doubts about orders still left. Had they been already? Had they forgotten?

By six the turkey was being plucked by Granny, but often the shop door was still open, waiting for the late-comers, and Mum and Dad were dead on their feet. Christmas at school in the infants usually meant weeks of making decorations and a party on the last day with everyone of us bringing something to put on the table. As I remember there was always an over-abundance of jelly, huge red and green jellies, with the odd blancmange dotted here and there, set across the line of desks pulled together end to end to get us all sat round, the line covered with various tablecloths carefully ironed by all the Mums, and overlapping diagonally so our legs fitted into the V-shape gaps. Despite all the flavours, the jellies all seemed to be raspberry, strawberry and lime, and the blancmange strawberry and vanilla. We once took a Wincarnis, which was purple, but it was avoided like it was poison because it was posh, so it was red or green after that.

The weeks leading up to it were a hive of activity as we were all put to making paper chains out of coloured paper. We seemed to make miles of them, due no doubt to the naughty boys pulling at them to tease us, and breaking them. They were hung across the ceiling in great swathes and around the walls, with pictures of snowmen done on blue sugar paper. It was very difficult to make a snowman white on blue sugar paper. Usually we stuck cotton wool on after pasting it with flour and water "glue". We stuck cotton wool on the windows too, but only with a bit of spit, leaving us a constant task every day of re-spitting it as it dropped off. The school Christmas party was the main event of our school year, sports day coming second, when we all ran with egg and spoon, and jumped about in sacks, and tied three legs together in the name of fun. It was too.

At Christmas all the games were inside, usually Musical Chairs when we got to push somebody off a chair without being told off, Pass the Parcel sitting cross-legged on the floor, and Pin the Tail on the Donkey. Santa came too, usually popping in looking like someone's Grandad with cotton wool stuck on his chin. We weren't fooled. We knew it wasn't the real Santa because he was too busy, sorting out Christmas Eve. We always got a present though, which we all swapped with one another until we were satisfied ours was the best one. Then the Mums turned up to help clean up all the dropped jelly, and find our labelled knives, forks and spoons, brought with the jelly and tablecloth wrapped in a paper carrier bag. Our homemade paper hats were taken home with them if they had survived, carefully folded in our hands, to be shown to Granny when she came and to wear on Christmas Day. When we moved up into the juniors, we still had a party, but there was no visit from Santa as we were deemed too old for all that, and had to make do with the games. We had to make little gifts for Mum and Dad too. Usually something out of felt, like a handkerchief case, blanket-stitched all round with wool. One year we made slippers with big pom-poms on, made by wrapping wool round a card. Mum was a dab hand at that, she made lovely pom-poms. The slippers didn't last long but they were good for toasting our feet

157

in front of the fire before they wore away on the coconut matting.

Despite all the preparations going on at home for Christmas, Mum would find time to Christmas-shop for us, sneaking out when she could in the afternoons and coming home to hide the presents in the wardrobe. We, like all children, had a list for Santa, but in those days money wasn't readily available to spend spoiling us. We didn't get what children get today. The norm was one big present and a few stocking fillers like colouring books and crayons. We always had a cut-out doll book, where we could cut out different outfits to change the doll's dress. We had hours of fun with those until the little paper flaps tore off with too much use. If we had had sellotape, they would have lasted twice as long. Tins of Sharps toffee were always in our pillowcase, too, along with an apple and an orange and a bag of chocolate coins, which we used for money in our games of "shop" until they were melted to the gold foil and no longer fit to eat. We always had a new skipping rope, too, although when a few of us played we used Mum's old washing line, which wasn't plastic coated in those days and was thrown away when it started to dirty the washing. There was usually a game and a jigsaw to fill up the pillowcase, which we left one on either side of the fireplace with a mince pie and a glass of sherry in the hearth for Santa and a carrot for the reindeer. When we dashed down stairs at six a.m. the next morning, there were only crumbs left and dirty footprints on the hearth, which we gazed at in awe before the serious stuff of ripping open the wrapping paper to see what he had brought. Our biggest ever present was a bicycle, which was second-hand and between us, causing endless trouble as we fought and squabbled over it all through the Christmas holidays, leaving Mum and Dad to referee as to whose turn it was to ride and whose it was to run behind. Before Easter appeared we were bought another to stop the fights. Unfortunately it caused more trouble because it was a snazzy Phillips red and metallic blue sports model which we both wanted to ride, the loser having to be content with the old black "sit up and beg" boneshaker and trundling on behind. When we asked for roller skates Mum made sure we had a pair each, remembering the number of fights over the bikes.

We always looked forward to our presents from Auntie Vera, who had a knack of knowing what we would like. More often than not it was a pretty dress each, made on her sewing machine. They were always dainty with the bodice smocked and embroidered, something Mum hadn't the time to do. One Christmas she knitted fluffy pink boleros that were the latest fashion and matched the dresses exactly. She was very clever with her hands and when she bought a knitting machine she kept us going in woollies for years.

It was always Granny who made the stuffing for the turkey on Christmas Eve after the shop had closed, with us helping to grate the stale bread, skin the sausages, and stir it to bind it all together. We also helped her to pluck out any remaining feathers as she sat with the bird held between her knees. It was a ritual part of Christmas after Dad had chopped off the head and neck. Then the stuffing was put inside the cavity and Granny sewed it up to stop it leaking out, and tied the legs together with string, ready for Dad to put it on a baking sheet in the bakehouse. The next morning, Christmas Day, it would be put in the oven with several others the neighbours had brought in to be roasted in the big oven. All had names on, then they didn't get mixed up. The hardest job was keeping the cat away. He would always appear when they came out of the oven, drawn by the smell I suppose, and once or twice, despite being chased off, managed to have a sly nibble. He was always drawn to Billy Pike's, it being the biggest, but once dragged a whole leg off the newsagent's, leaving us to explain it that had come off in the cooking. He was very nice about it, but the cat wasn't too pleased after Dad had chased it round the bakehouse twice brandishing the sweeping brush, and out into the cold back street for the day in punishment.

Once all the turkeys had been picked up, we sat down to our Christmas dinner, which in those days was a simpler affair. We never had posh starters or wine, but we did set the Christmas pudding on fire with rum poured on by Mum, Dad lighting it with a match to great cheers all round. Granny always washed up, with us helping to wipe in our small kitchen. There wasn't much room, so we took it in turns with the tea towel, putting the pots away in the yellow kitchenette as we wiped. We had no best pots as we do now, so if we dropped them, it didn't really matter. Mum just bought more from the Progress Stores across the road, and not posh ones; they were never in a set. By the time we had done, Mum and Dad would be dozing in front of the fire, so Granny usually shooed us off to play in the bakehouse. Often all three were asleep, with Granny snoring, when we crept in for anything, the radio and the Queen blaring out in vain. TV wasn't an issue, we didn't have one, so we made our own amusement while the adults dozed and had a quiet day. In the evening we played games after tea, with Mum and Dad joining in. Granny usually listened to the radio in front of the fire. She was very into *The Archers*, and *Mrs. Dale's Diary*, and we all listened to A1 Read and *Life with the Lyons*. Granny being "chapel", she never went to church on Christmas Day. Fletcher Street Methodists just wasn't the same.

After the quietness of Christmas Day, we were usually asked to Auntie Vera's on Boxing Day, setting off early with Granny between us in the back seat, feet astride the drive shaft and knees up to her chin. Over Blackstone Edge and up the road leading in to Horsforth, to call at Auntie Phyllis's first to thank her for our presents, and then on to Auntie Vera's in time for our dinner, edging into the kitchen to the clatter of natter and a good smell of dinner. The house would always be full. Dad's Auntie Grace and Grandma Toothill sat one either side of the fireplace, Uncle Lawrence's mother, who we called "yer knaw" for her usage of these two words on the end of every sentence, and her sister Ida, complete with husband Uncle Jim who squired them about, sat three in a row squashed into a small settee. Often there was Uncle Lawrence's sister, Auntie Olga, and her husband and daughter Pat

161

there too, but we all managed to fit in, sitting on borrowed chairs or cross-legged on the rug, while Auntie Vera and Uncle Lawrence dished out the dinner and passed the plates round the two tables in various sittings. We were all urged to get stuck in, and not wait until everyone was served, which Mum always said was rude because it was manners to wait until everyone was served before we could start. If we had waited, all the delicious food would have been cold, so when they received a plate everyone tucked in there and then. The washing up was monumental, and went on till nearly teatime at times, with all the adults taking a turn, and a lot of laughter coming from the kitchen in the process as gossip was caught up on here and there. While the adults were washing up we kids played games, digging out the Snakes and Ladders and Ludo. Occasionally we played Beetle, which was popular at the time, waiting to throw a six before we could get the body to start. At teatime the whole process of feeding us started again, with little sandwiches and Auntie Vera's special sausage rolls which had the odd silver threepenny bit wrapped in greaseproof paper hidden in the sausage meat. Today it would be regarded as dangerous and unhygienic, I suppose, but it never did us any harm, and a shriek of delight would go up on discovering them. Mum and Dad usually helped out with whist pies brought from home and fancy cakes to be put on plates with a lacy doily. There was always a big trifle laced with sherry and loaded with fresh cream too, made by Mum, I presume, that made us kids tipsy. After tea we all played Pass the Parcel, Pin the Tail on the Donkey and other parlour games popular in Mum and Dad's time as children, with all the Grandmas and Great Aunts joining in, memories of their youthful times being trotted out here and there.

We all had lovely times at their house at Christmas. Our present Christmases with television and expensive presents seem positively dull in comparison, and seem to have "lost the plot" when it comes down to simple enjoyment, and good family company. We tried hard to make it last as long as we could, but after begging for "a bit longer", the time would eventually come when the coats were brought forth and warmed in front of the fire to be put on, our goodbyes said and all cheeks kissed, our thank yous given, prizes gathered up and empty dishes put in the car. Then it was home to Bolton, Christmas over for another year, and work for Mum and Dad in the morning. Granny came with us to stay for another week sometimes, but often we dropped her at home in a cold dark house, to light her fire to warm up the rooms, and reflect on us all and the times we had, and tell Auntie Phyllis of the hectic rush in the run up to Christmas. New Year's Eve usually saw us at the army barracks in Fletcher Street to do the New Years Eve dance. There was lots of drunkenness of course, but it was generally merry and good humoured. I don't recall any fights, though it was rowdy with everyone out for a good time. After the posh buffet had been served and cleared up, we went on to the balcony to watch the dancing and see the raffle drawn, Mum hopefully holding the raffle tickets waiting for the numbers to be drawn out. There were some good boxes

163

of chocolates which we all had our eyes on, large boxes with a fancy picture on the front. When we did manage to win one, the box would be kept for our crayons and pencils once the chocolates had gone, giving the scent of chocolate off till the smell of crayon took over and the lid was dog-eared and faded with use. We all joined in Auld Lang Syne at midnight, and then the stuff would be put in the car, with Mum and us and the Farrs walking the short distance home, sometimes in a line continuing the conga, to save Dad an extra journey. Or was it for Dad to let in the New Year, which Mum always insisted on, because he was the only one with dark hair?

Everything seemed quiet after Christmas and New Year, with only the fairground to look forward to, and we waited for the bad weather to set in, giving us some snow. We went back to school, but it never seemed long before the dark nights abated and spring appeared. Easter was never long in coming either, when huge blocks of chocolate appeared in the bakehouse, ready for Dad's Easter eggs, when they were melted down in the oven and swirled generously around egg moulds and left to set. As they set, we would hover round, knowing they were fiddly to remove and that Dad would let us feast on the broken bits until they sickened us. We would get a telling off from Mum if we were sick, and Dad too for the lack of common sense in letting us eat so much, which was even worse, because "the children don't know any better". As Easter drew nearer the novelty of so much chocolate wore off, and we helped him stick the two sides together, melting the flat sides on a hot baking sheet and putting them on a tray to be decorated with Easter chicks and sugar flowers. As they were ordered to be picked up on Easter Saturday, he piped children's names on them, and would even place a small gift in them if one was brought in by the customer. They were very popular, and as with the mince pies at Christmas finished up in our bedroom between covered trays, stacked in the corners and every available space. It was chocolate heaven, because the smell pervaded everywhere despite the covering trays. Soon the Easter fancies appeared as well. But it wasn't like Christmas. These were decorated with small nests of eggs and chicks, and weren't as rich or as varied as Christmas ones. Still, the marzipan eggs were lovely and a change from chocolate. It was a bit hard to keep out of the boxes at times, although Dad didn't seem to mind.

I think cakes were more popular then. Mum sold loads of them, displaying them on little round cake stands in the window. Everyone had a posh cake stand. You don't see them today, only in teashops, but then they were in common use. Mum's were all in cut glass, each with a clean crisp white doily, set in groups in the window bottom out of the reach of little hands, apart from ours that is, when we would stand for ages making up our mind which to have with our tea. Hot cross buns would start to appear the week before Easter, unlike today when you can buy them all year round. Dad's were in a triangular shape to represent the Trinity. They were full of fruit and peel, and had a rich dark spicy flavour, and a sticky dark glaze tasting of cinnamon and mixed spices. Today's manufactured variety are a pale imitation. When Easter comes I long for one of Dad's, and remember fondly the days we spent making them. All lined up at the bakehouse table, we rolled and folded till we were fit only to drop, revived with cups of tea to plough on, rolling and folding, rolling and folding, and placing them on baking trays to rise in Dad's steam prover before they were baked in the oven to a rich golden brown and glazed and stood up on trays, ready to be taken through to the shop. Mum took orders all the week before, and "Hot Cross Bun Day" dawned bright and early to a hive of activity that saw Dad working all the night before. We started about four o'clock, with a first cup of the hot sweet tea that kept us going, interspersed with a few samples of Hot Cross Buns all day. The heady spicy smell permeated the house and shop, and spread into the street, sending passers-by in to join the queue for a hot and buttered bun, fresh from the oven, to eat on their way to town, calling in on their way back for another and a dozen or so to take home for the family.

The Thursday before Easter and Christmas Eve were the busiest days of the year for Mum and Dad, but Good Friday if the weather was good saw us join the annual trek "up the Pike", a Bolton tradition. Rivington is now a country park and was recently used as the cross-country course for the Commonwealth Games. Once it was the home of Lord Leverhulme, who built the Sunlight Soap empire and Port Sunlight on Merseyside. He surrounded his bungalow home with tiered gardens and follies on the edge of the moors above Horwich, a few miles from Bolton and now the home of the Reebok Stadium, built to replace Burnden Park, Bolton's football stadium, demolished a few years ago. The house no longer stands but the foundations are still there and can be seen among the overgrown rhododendrons that have run amok over the site. The Pike is a stone folly in the shape of a keep on top of a huge mound, which looks man-made. It can be seen for miles around, standing like a fortress, the well-worn path brown among the grass, like a scar up one side. On Good Friday hundreds of people make the climb, a tradition going back generations; it was the Good Friday day out. When we used to go in the 1950s, there were refreshment stands and people selling things, all out to make a bob or two out of the day. It all added to the attraction of "going up't'Pike", and many families took a picnic, spreading out a rug to sit on and making a day of it, with extra transport laid on to and from the Pike.

Saturday, it was back to work for Mum and Dad, with the shop open for the bread, and fare for Easter Sunday and Monday. Easter would see us with a new dress apiece and new shoes, for our Easter outing to Buxton and Matlock Bath where we always seemed to go. Easter was always the time for our "long walk" too, to "break in our new shoes", and was regarded by Jean as child cruelty. Especially in new shoes. One Easter we caught the bus to Egerton, and walked the several miles of Longworth Clough over the moors to Belmont and the Blue Lagoon, a small reservoir, and picnic area, notorious in summer for skinny dipping. Jean cried almost the whole way, with little sympathy from Mum and Dad who thought it a huge joke until they saw the size of the blisters caused by the new shoes as the blood-soaked socks were peeled off at home. When Mum patched them up with Germolene and large plasters, she cried even harder as the Germolene penetrated the raw flesh. They took ages to heal, and Longworth Clough received a notoriety in our family. We never ventured there again, only in the car, remembering the pride in the new shoes and the pain of the blisters to follow.

With Easter gone, the days started to get longer and, after the closed-in nights of winter spent hugging the fire and blocking out the draughts, we started to venture out after tea when the shop had closed. Dad dug out his fishing tackle to fish in the reservoirs on the moors above Bolton, while we played on the bank, poking homemade "boats" of twigs with a stick to make them go faster in races along the reservoir bank. Mum would sit with Dad, watching the fishing, and reading a book. It wasn't as good as Pooh Sticks with matches in the gutter, because they didn't get caught up on gunge, and a wrong move with the stick sent them spiralling out of reach and then losing the race. After a while we would be rounded up and bribed into the car, with the promise of a bag of chips from the chip shop near the Royal Oak in Bradshaw, where we could eat them out of the newspaper, sitting on the kerb. Mum and Dad imbibed a half shandy and a pint of beer respectively, brought out by Dad on a tin tray. Other times we would go to pick bluebells and primroses,

168

bringing them home in great handfuls to put in jam jars around the house. It was lovely, once we had a car, to get out of the terraced streets and into the countryside on the lighter nights in spring. We took Graham too, all piling into the back seat behind Mum and Dad, to run amok for a while in the fresh air.

After the summer holidays, our next highlight of the year was Bonfire Night. For weeks before the kids of Bolton would forage for wood, not easy in a built-up area like ours where most people had coal fires, and firewood was always in short supply; so much so that Mum would twist old newspaper into "firelighters", knotting the folded twisted paper to make it burn longer to get the fire going. Things that were scavenged were old gateposts and any rotten bits of boardings that edged properties awaiting demolition. Old chairs and settees were prized items; anyone who promised these for Bonfire Night expected to get an errand or two done in exchange for weeks. Anything that wasn't nailed down disappeared quickly as the streets were scavenged for anything that would burn. It was all stockpiled in someone's back yard until the appointed day. Often there was filching of stockpiles, done in the dark nights, and rows broke out between rival bonfires, each street guarding its own pile zealously during the last week. The pilfering of old mill skips was rife, as they vanished to reappear on someone's bonfire surreptitiously under a pile of scavenged settees, their owners usually unaware of their valuable contribution to the street bonfire. Mum never let us make a Guy, as she said it was begging, but most kids did, sitting by it in doorways and begging a penny from each passer by. We hoped for a dry night, as rain made it difficult to get the fire going, but it did seem to be wet a lot on Bonfire Night. Dad, much to Mum's dismay, would chuck on a bit of paraffin, standing well back as he tossed on a bit of burning newspaper. Cotton waste soaked in methylated spirits was another of his solutions. Dangerous as it may seem, it always did the trick and we all stood well back. The whole street joined in, everyone bringing something to make a real feast. Black peas with vinegar warmed us on cold nights, and hot potatoes, burned black where we had chucked them at the edge of the fire to the point of being inedible. They were usually raw on the inside but we ate them anyway, with a good shake of salt, which made our chapped lips, acquired in the endless hunt for wood, smart.

Mum made her special treacle toffee, which she sold in the shop, in paper bags which were reluctant to give up their goodies. Black and stuck to the paper, we peeled it or sucked it off, whichever was the case, and kept it in our pockets, a bag each, to be savoured in between the constant flow of Bonfire Night fare dished up at intervals throughout the night. We hovered as she made it, dipping fingers into the black treacle as she tried to measure it in tablespoons and transfer the sticky stuff into the pan. Once all in, with the "best" butter and sugar, it was stirred with a wooden spoon to keep it from burning, each of us taking a turn and trying to avoid the splashes as it bubbled away in the pan, testing the drops at regular intervals in the saucer of cold water to see if it was brittle enough to be declared "done" and poured into the tin to set, and impatient for it to be ready. Well-broken with Dad's hammer into mouth-size pieces and weighed into quarters, we didn't always get it right. Our cheeks bulged with the oversize pieces, leaving Mum to break it up further to make it look more for the money. She did a roaring trade, selling it with Dad's Parkin in a job lot.

Dad's Parkin was the best. Everybody said so, coming for it as soon as it appeared in the shop window to "make sure" of it. Made in great slabs and sticky on top, it was dark and delicious. Mum would weigh it out into squares and put a price ticket on in the shop window. Some came back for more, unable to resist the delightful stuff. It was a huge joke that it made you "run", and Mum and Dad used to joke about the extra toilet paper given free with every slab. There's no doubt about it, it was a great bowel mover, and the old ladies of Granny's age, who were a generation somewhat obsessed with their bowels, used to turn up in droves as soon as it appeared, much to Mum and Dad's delight and profit margin. It was commented on too by the cheekier ones, and toilet jokes abounded in the shop all week, sending us all into fits of laughter as we listened, ear to the shop curtain and hiding in the cupboard under the stairs. It was even worth the odd crack of a cockroach as we jostled to hear all the cheeky talk going on. We were relieved too, in more ways than one. It was much nicer than the "Syrup of Figs" Mum insisted on dosing us with at regular intervals, in the unending attempts to keep us "regular".

We were quite sorry when Bonfire Night was over, and the "fireworks", in more ways than one. The fireworks were usually bought loose from Mr. Doherty's, the newsagent on the next block. Displayed in a glass case, you could pick your own. They were quite noisy ones, particularly the penny bangers and jumping jacks, which the boys had a bad habit of throwing at girls to make them shriek. They were dangerous if they went down your wellies, so we tried to stay out of the way if strangers appeared on the night as some did. Some boys went round bonfires. They were given food too, everyone was welcome. When the fireworks were half over, the potato pie was dished out. We stood around the bonfire eating it, with red cabbage which always accompanied it, the heat from the fire warming our faces and the hot potato pie warming our insides, but our feet remaining frozen despite the wellies and the two pairs of socks. The biggest rockets were always kept till last, with the Catherine wheels being stuck on the mill shutters with a pin and let off at regular intervals. We must have burned the paint off the shutters now and again, but no-one complained to my knowledge. If they did, Dad never told us. The Pikes kept a low profile too; they were a bit too posh, or thought they were, to join in. As the night tapered to an end all too soon, the Mums chased us all in, protesting at the unfairness, as the Dads were allowed to shovel the hot embers into the cinder pit at the top of the street. All smoky, and faces smeared with smuts and dirt, we sat at either end of the bath while Mum scrubbed away the smoke and smuts with the loofah, and peeled any remaining toffee from our pocket linings. Then we were hurried into bed, to dream of the good time had by all.

We never managed to burn down the mill, or had any accidents, apart from the occasional burned fingers from the hot metal of the sparklers. The smoky smell hung about the streets for days, and any good housewife refrained from changing her net curtains until after Bonfire Night had gone. The smoke and fog eventually cleared, as did our sore throats from inhaling the smoke. Still, a good time was had by all and that's what counted.

CHAPTER
NINE

Summer Holidays

When we started to take the Wakes Weeks holidays, most of them were taken with Aunties and Uncles, and Grandmas and Grandads. We stayed in caravans mostly, but occasionally Mum and Dad were flushed, allowing us to stay in boarding houses. They usually proved such disasters Dad refused to stay in them after a while. His brushes with domineering seaside landladies became legendary. We had a disastrous week in Morecambe, staying in a particularly run-down establishment. The poor food and shabby bedroom had a depressing effect and, after a week of bad weather and poor food, he put his foot down firmly, and refused point blank to go in one again. We weren't surprised. After a week of trailing round in the rain and trying to find something to do, we all returned home worse for wear, tempers frayed and wishing we had stayed at home. The trouble was most landladies in those days liked to be rid of you by ten o'clock. It wasn't done to be in during the day, rain or not; it disturbed their well-ordered routine. Very few places we stayed in had a lounge, or indeed anywhere to sit if it was raining. They had a few bedrooms to let and a dining room. There

174

was not much of a welcome either in some of the places, and a list of dos and don'ts on the back of the bedroom door, that read like the Ten Commandments. Worst of all was the food, and they had the cheek to charge for "use of the cruet" to improve the taste of the stodge. Despite the landladies, and Mum and Dad's attempts at keeping down our noise, we had some good holidays in Morecambe even though the beach wasn't ideal for sand pies. What sand there was was usually crowded when the weather was nice, but it wasn't a place to tuck your dress in your knickers to paddle, as the sea was usually nowhere in sight for most of the time. Apart from the swing boats which were located on the prom behind, we made good use of the mechanical elephant that clanked near the stone jetty. The only entertainment on the beach in those days was getting to grips with putting up a deck chair in which to park Granny, while Mum and Dad took regular walks up and down the prom to kill the boredom. When we were all thoroughly bored, Granny with being sandblasted and deafened by the mechanical elephant, and us with picking the squelching mud from between our toes, Mum and Dad turned up puzzled as to what to do with us all next. The last year, after the week in the dire establishment in Morecambe, the landlady severely stepped out of line, suggesting we bring fish and chips in. She offered to serve them on plates, with tea, bread and butter, but as we were staying bed and board it was cheek to say the least. Dad was furious, and we left the next day. After that we stayed in caravans. Besides being cheaper, they gave us more freedom and a chance to

175

take advantage of all that sea air, something we didn't get in Bolton. When the weather was bad we weren't thrown out to tramp the prom, something Dad was eternally grateful for.

Bolton Wakes Weeks ran from the last Friday in June and the first in July, when a mass exodus took place. The mills shut down their engines and any necessary maintenance work to the mills was done in those two weeks. Local shops closed and the streets emptied. Those who couldn't afford the weeks away had to shop in the town centre, which normally stayed open to some extent. The market was open in Ashburner Street, and was always crowded those two weeks, with people who normally didn't get to use it flocking in from the outlying areas where most of the shops were closed. Bolton Market Hall had some shops open, but most were closed. The doors were open, though, to give access to the few that were. Even so it wasn't quite the same. When Dad bought the shop, we closed just the first week and opened the second. Later on, he decided to close the full two weeks and we always went away, taking Granny after Grandad had died. Mum and Dad could go off on their own if they wanted, with Granny to look after us, but mostly we all stayed together at the caravan site or going out in the car to see places. If the weather was good, the beach was our first choice, with Dad going to fish off the rocks when the tide was right. We helped him dig the bait off the beach, leaving great gaping holes till the tide came in to fill them in.

Some of the caravans were pretty basic in those days, with Jean and me having beds made up on the floor in some of them. Mum and Dad slept on the double bed made by dropping the table across the bench seats and putting the backrest cushions down to make the mattress. Granny slept on the single bench seat, which can't have been very comfy, but we all managed to sleep somewhere, floor or not. There were no toilets in them, we had to "go" in the field toilet block, which also had washbasins. There wasn't much privacy; it was a case of mucking in literally, especially when we had a farm caravan in the middle of nowhere. Once we had a caravan with an infestation of ants. They were everywhere. Mum had brought some of Dad's chocolate cake and despite the tin lid on the biscuit tin, they ate more than we did. You couldn't tell them from the chocolate strands, they were so thick. They certainly enjoyed the chocolate butter cream, and we left them fatter for our visit.

Sometimes we holidayed with Auntie Vera and Uncle Lawrence, renting caravans at Benllech Bay on Anglesey. It was very wet one week, with mud ankle deep on the site. Susan was very young and Ann was just a baby, so they had afternoon naps which didn't go down all that well with Dad who cleared off to fish in the little cove on his own. Uncle Lawrence and Dad decided to go fishing in the bay, but their attempts to rent a little boat came to naught as the boatman found one excuse after another to deter them. His main excuse was "No bait, sir," spoken in a sing-song Welsh accent which Dad never forgot, using it in later years when he wanted to deter us from doing something without actually saying no. We knew what he meant.

177

Despite being shore-bound, Dad and Uncle Lawrence caught plenty of fish for Mum to fry for supper and kept the campsite supplied all week.

It took ages to get to Wales on all the country roads and we had to meet Auntie Vera and family on the way. That was a work of art in itself as our rendezvous were often delayed by breakdowns. Eventually we would meet to tell the sorry tale, often after the AA man had patched one or the other (usually us) at the side of the road. Then we would travel together, in the hope of not getting lost in the poorly signposted town centres. Once we went round Bristol three times, taking the wrong road each time, and returning to the same roundabout, which was a source of great amusement to the three of us but not to Dad. Auntie Vera's box Brownie recorded much of it, with the whole family, kids in front "watching for the birdie", huge grins on our faces apart from Susan who hated the camera. One of our snaps was taken in an old stagecoach in the middle of Wales. All ten of us are piled on top, grinning like Cheshire cats. They were often trotted out at Christmas with the memories they brought back when the subject of holidays came up. As we all got better off, Auntie Vera and Uncle Lawrence bought a tiny caravan, which at first they kept in their back garden. Mum and Dad bought an old army ridge tent, having nowhere to keep a caravan. God forbid the rows Dad would have had with Mr. Pike if a caravan had appeared in the back street. We would set up a little colony on various holidays in the second half of the 1950s, when Granny started going to Skegness with one of her friends.

We were always amazed at the amount of stuff they brought with them as it all came out of the car and caravan. They seemed to corner the market in windbreakers and picnic rugs, giving us lots of fun as they unpacked, leaving us wondering what would come out next. Not like us. Our first attempt at camping had us sleeping on the floor on a ground sheet. Admittedly we all had ex-army sleeping bags, but I wouldn't recommend the experience. Dad pitched the tent on a hillside, and, as you can probably guess, we had all rolled to one side of the tent in the night, me with my nose on the cold canvas and practically underneath them all. So much for Dad's camping experience. We had to admit it was fun when the weather was warm, and we soon acquired camp beds to sleep on, and a camp kettle. Then we bought a job lot of camping equipment second-hand from the ads page in the Bolton *Evening News*. This included a table with detachable screw legs, and two chairs and two canvas stools. All this comfort gave us quite a big problem as other things were added to it like a lantern and a roll of carpet in the effort to make it like home. Mum didn't know where to stop, and Dad had to buy a second-hand trailer to put it all in. In the end it took us longer to unpack than Auntie Vera's family, and our army camp roughing it became cosseted luxury. We must have looked ridiculous as we rolled out the wall-to-wall carpet and put it in a tent. We even wiped our feet as we came in, reluctant to bring in the mud. It all nearly came to a sad end, too, as the second-hand trailer unhooked itself on the Queensferry bypass, and overtook us, diving into a field and finishing up in a hedge. Luckily no-one was hurt and the road was empty at the time. Still, it was a hairy experience and Dad tied it on with good stout washing line after that to make doubly sure it was secured fast.

As the continental tents became available, Mum and Dad got rid of the old ridge tent and bought one of those second-hand. It was fairly new and quite large, and took us ages to put up the first time. It was French and like most things French had bits of mould here and there. It had a built-in ground sheet too, to keep out the creepy crawlies, so the wall-to-wall carpet had to go. We got rid of the old camp kettle as well. It was a pain in the neck, even worse than Mum's Tilly lamp and that's saying something. It consisted of a tube of metal with a double skin, in between which you poured the water. There was a cavity at the bottom in which you built a fire of twigs, the theory being the fire boiled the water. As theories go, this was a non-starter as the twigs were always green, or wet, or both. It could take a good half hour and half a tree to get the water hot, and there was often more smoke than fire. Dad would revert to his usual tactic of "chucking on a bit of paraffin" after messing about for ages with bits of newspaper and kneeling down "blowing" into the blessed thing. It produced more smoke than hot water, and got us into hot water with other campers who had a Camping Gaz ring, and a clean air policy.

Camping Gaz was a godsend, and our camping left Dad's pre-war boy scouts and moved into the twentieth century, where it took only a few minutes to make a cup of tea. Despite all the modernisation, we still managed a few hairy moments here and there. Once we camped under power lines in a field. With hindsight, not very wise. During a tremendous thunderstorm in the middle of the night, the lines started to spark across and smoulder. Mum dragged us out of bed, fearing for our lives. The storm went on for ages as we sat in the safety of the car across the field watching it. Dad, who was never one to lose out on sleep, decided we had better move the tent as it could go on all night. We carried all the stuff out in the pouring rain, and put it in the trailer. Then Dad whipped out the tent pegs, and we all took a corner each inside the tent and carried it, marching across the field in unison, as far away from the power lines as we could get. God help anyone watching that night who had had one over the eight if they saw a tent grow eight "feet" and walk across a field. We left all the stuff in the trailer as it was all soaked, and got back in our sleeping bags, wet pyjamas piled in a heap in the corner of the tent. The next morning we sorted it all out and laughed off the experience, but we never camped under power lines again; it made us very wary of them, and the danger.

We had some lovely camping holidays over the years. Everyone was very friendly, as campers are, sitting outside the tent at night swapping camping tales, watching the sun go down and batting off the midges. We went to Devon and Cornwall a lot, staying at different places. We managed to see most of the coastline over the years, but the journey down was horrendous. It often took twelve hours to get there,

181

having to go through most town centres in the absence of motorways. We even went overnight in the effort to beat the rush, but it was still busy because everyone else seemed to have the same idea. There were some terrible traffic jams, even in those days, but nowhere near today's snarl ups. Our car would boil regularly, and we always had a pop bottle in the back seat to top up the radiator, sitting on the side of the road with the bonnet up, waiting for it to cool down so Dad could loosen the radiator cap and pour in the water. Then the dreadful business would start all over again, stopping and starting all the way to Bristol and Taunton, the two notorious bottlenecks.

We were the signpost spotters, sitting in the back seat, bored to death and anxious to be there. It was Dad's way of keeping us amused, looking for the signposts. Then it was who could spot the sea first, when a huge cheer would go up. By then the sandwiches would be long gone, and we would all be starving, and grumpy, the novelty of I Spy worn off and legs cramped and full of "the Nadgers", unable to keep still and taking swipes at each other in the back seat. After twelve hours in the car the tent still had to be put up, Mum organising us, and dishing out the jobs. Jean always "volunteered" to put up the camp beds, and roll out the sleeping bags. Later, when we decided the camp beds were cold to sleep on, she blew up the Lilos while we all put up the tent. Then someone was sent for water and had to find the nearest tap. The sites varied, and some of the ones we stayed on, like Maen Valley, are still there today. Most had washing facilities and a little

182

shop for basics and a newspaper. As camping took off, the sites got better and we didn't feel as though we were roughing it. We were, of course, even if we had the wall-to-wall carpet and then a posh tent. When it rained, it was awful as the fields turned into muddy quagmires, difficult to get on and off. But we stuck it out, in macs and wellies, and a grim hope it would brighten up sooner or later. It usually did, of course, and we would come home brown as berries anyway with being in the fresh air all the time.

Pulling down the tent and packing everything away in the rain was a nightmare; all wet through and the tent heavy with the accumulated water. It wasn't finished there either. When we got home, it all had to be dried out to stop the canvas rotting. Dad unpacked it with our help, and then it had to be spread out in the bakehouse in front of the oven to dry, turning it over every so often to dry out the various bits. Luckily this performance wasn't often, and we tried to beat the rain, knowing the performance we would have if we didn't. Any dampness left in the tent would end up as mould and, on our next excursion, the tent would reek of mushrooms and be wearing a fur coat.

Quite a few of our holidays were spent in Wales, especially if Dad was brassed off at the thought of the long journey "down south". It was easier to get to and a lot quieter. Conway and Tenby were our favourite spots, and Aberystwyth, where we camped at the side of the river, a short distance from the town centre. The beaches were good, and clean, with crystal clear water. Borth, near Aberystwyth, was where we could have the beach to ourselves, it was so quiet, and the sand was fine and golden with no litter at all. Conway was where we went most of all. The beach wasn't as good, but Llandudno was nearby and the town was pretty. We stayed at Morfa Nefyn, where the road tunnel is today. Then it was sand dunes, with caravans between the dunes. Dad fished off the rocks at the far end towards Penmaenmawr, catching pollock and whiting with worms dug in the Conway estuary. We spent time in the Lido at Deganwy too. It was open air, so the weather had to be good because the water was freezing. Nevertheless it was cheap to go in and safe to swim, whereas the beach at Conway had strong currents. It was a long way from today's water park standards, but had a shelving shallow end, where the water warmed up in the sun, making it pleasant to splash about in. Very different from the cockroach-ridden baths at High Street, where we learned to swim.

Dad made use of the deep diving pool. He was an excellent swimmer, going way out of his depth, causing Mum to worry when we were on the beach and he disappeared half a mile out. Our days there passed pleasantly, with the Lido, the beach, and Dad's fishing excursions. Granny was usually with us too. One year we were glad of her company, when Dad disappeared for a full day on one of his fishing excursions, leaving Mum very worried as to his whereabouts. He had decided to try his luck salmon fishing as a change from fishing from the rocks. He had heard of a little spot where the fishing was good and, packing some lunch, disappeared with the rods in the car to a little Welsh village on a salmon river. Mum and Granny decided to spend the day on the beach and waved him off expecting him and a salmon back for teatime. By ten o'clock that night he hadn't returned, and they were both extremely worried for his safety, not even knowing where he had gone. As midnight approached they were just discussing whether or not to call the police and all the hospitals, fearing he had come to grief somewhere, when he turned up. Nonchalant as always, he had decided to try a bit of night fishing, having had no luck during the day, buying fish and chips for his tea. Thinking Mum and Granny might be worried about his absence hadn't occurred to him. Glad as they were to see he was all right, and after listening to the excuses, Mum and Granny "let him have it", and he was well chastised. The next time he fancied a bit of salmon fishing, we all went with him. For all the trouble, and his efforts, the salmon eluded him. The only salmon we saw that week was out of a tin, but to give Dad his due, it wasn't for want of trying. That day went down in family history as "the day Dad disappeared in Wales". Mum and Granny never let him forget it.

Abersoch was another of our holiday spots, where we rented a caravan on the Warren. Set in the sand dunes on the beach it was teeming with rabbits, and when we knew it, it was very quiet. There were more rabbits than people, and they were very tame, hopping round the caravans early in the morning before anyone was up and about. Needless to say the sand dunes were littered with their droppings, but it didn't detract from the site; they gave the place a bit of character, and the children

185

loved them. Abersoch had a lovely clean beach, with soft white sand which we made ample use of as the weather always seemed to be good. It was nothing like it is today, the beach badly churned up with boats and tractors, and caravans and chalets galore in among the sand dunes. The little shop has turned into a takeaway heaving with folk, and smelling of chips. Progress, I suppose. The little pub in the village where Mum and Dad wet their whistles is hardly recognisable, and isn't a quiet little pub any more. Now it is a well-known holiday spot, and has all the paraphernalia to go with it. We turned brown as berries on the beach, after the initial sunburn had faded from a bright red. Suntan lotion wasn't a requisite then as it is now, and our tender young skins turned pink and then red in no time at all. When that happened the damage was done, leaving us to suffer the agonies of burnt backs after a day on the beach. Awareness of the danger always came too late, leaving Mum with the option of Nivea Cream or Calamine lotion to soothe the fire in our skin, dabbing it on gently with bits of cotton wool to our oohs and aaghs at the pressure of the cotton wool and the coldness of the Calamine lotion. We had to dunk ourselves in the sea to ease the burning, leaving our skin tight and smarting with the salt. But it did take the pain of it away for a short while. Dad had no such trouble. He soon turned a dark chocolate colour, the legacy of his days in Burma in the war. His skin, accustomed to the sun, turned freckly quickly without burning like us. When we were very young we were made to wear sunbonnets with a frill at the back to protect our necks, but as we got older we considered it babyish, and quickly took them off, hoping it wasn't noticed by Mum. Lots of our early holiday snaps show us with buckets and spades and a windmill, clad in the infernal sun bonnets and knitted woollen bathing costumes. Later on we wore elasticated ones, which gathered up the cotton material to fit our bodies. Both were uncomfortable and scratchy and, when wet, sagged, allowing the sand to get in. After a day on the wet sand, the skin on our bottoms rubbed raw. The chapped bums and burned backs did nothing to lessen our pleasure of the beach, though, and we were ready for off again at the crack of dawn the next day.

We saw much of the country in those early years, as Mum and Dad took holidays in different areas, all at the seaside. It just wasn't done to go abroad. You had to be pretty rich to do that. Graham and the Farrs went to the Isle of Man for their holiday one year. In those years that was abroad. We still considered Devon and Cornwall as the ultimate destination. It seemed another world to us after the industrial northwest. We indulged heavily in cream teas, and anyone would have thought we weren't used to cream, despite the fact that Dad bought it in gallons for the bakehouse. Smiles filling our faces with delight at the mention of a cream tea, off we would set in search of the best. It wasn't always easy, and we made the best effort to find the prettiest tea garden and the best cream tea in the West Country. It was always a bit of a mystery as to how to eat it; to put the cream on first, and then the jam, or the other way round. Either way we couldn't go wrong, they were

187

delicious. Then there was the farmhouse cider, sold at the farmhouse on some of the sites we visited, which made Mum tiddly. It was cloudy and rough, and you had to take your own jug to be filled from the barrel. It made for many a night of laughter as we sat outside the tent, with Mum and Dad getting tiddlier with each glass. In Wales, we picked Pembroke new potatoes from the fields. Left in the ground and missed in the harvest, they were delicious with lots of butter for our tea. Dad bought Barra Brith, a sweet tea bread, to try, baking it at home to sell in the shop a time or two, but people didn't know what it was in Bolton and it was viewed with suspicion, all preferring Dad's big round teacakes instead. Foreign foods, even from Wales, weren't tried like they are now, so little was known about them.

Our holidays in September were usually taken at Morecambe. With only a week it seemed far enough to go. The illuminations were on by then, not as good as at Blackpool but the display at Happy Mount Park was usually a good show. We never went to Blackpool. I think the two years of living there had taken the shine off going there for holidays. Dad usually went to Cleveleys to fish, though, and caught some good codling in winter, while we did our best to keep ourselves amused, coming back to the car to thaw out occasionally. By September it was a bit cold for camping and the nights were drawing in, so we stayed in a boarding house. Dad gritted his teeth, and buckled under, leaving the fishing tackle in the car and doing his best not to tramp in the mud on the landlady's hall carpet when he had been out to dig the bait. We went to fish at Arnside, which is lovely in autumn, with the trees changing colour. We gathered blackberries to bring home on the last day for a blackberry and apple duff. The trees were full of crab apples, which grew wild in some places. We watched the bore rushing up the estuary. The autumn high tides often made it three feet or more, so it was very spectacular at that time of year. It could be dangerous too, as it came in fast, swirling around the arches of the railway bridge, and sweeping through at an enormous speed. Dad caught lots of dabs there, standing on the railway bridge wall when the tide was high.

When it rained, we went into Morecambe or to Heysham Head. It had a zoo and bits of amusements and a circus. There was also a little café in the main street that made its own nettle beer. That was always a must, sitting on the bench outside, with a glass of nettle beer each. It wasn't alcoholic, not then anyway, and they served us whether it was or not. Dad used to kid us it was by walking tiddly down the street. I don't think he was too keen on it, but Mum being a "quack" said it got a "road through her", and we all had to suffer the same fate. One of the occasions of the week was the "Miss United Kingdom" heats for Morecambe. We never missed that, watching all the beauty queens parading around the open air swimming baths. There was always someone famous to judge it too. We saw film stars and pop singers there such as David Whitfield and Frankie Vaughan. There were never any feminist objectors either.

189

Some Septembers we spent the holiday in Auntie Vera's caravan in Saltburn. We had some nice weeks there, although it was usually a bit nippy with the North Sea on the doorstep. Even in summer the sea was freezing, and the sea fret would roll in occasionally making it even more cold. There was a long prom, perfect for roller skating, and a pier with amusements where we spent most of our holiday money. The walk from the caravan was down a ravine, which was heavily wooded and had a stream running through it, much as it is today, but then it seemed a long way and we were loaded up with all the beach paraphernalia. We always needed a windbreak, even though Dad would moan about carrying it down and back. When we were there with Auntie Vera's family, we took everything down to the beach; flasks, food, picnic rugs, everything. It was like a flitting, all of us loaded up, walking down the little ravine which was dappled with sunlight and cool. We set up camp on the beach, hemmed in by the windbreaks, all the flasks and food in the coolest spot when the weather was warm. The wind off the sea was often blowing up the sand, so it got into everything. We spent all day there sometimes, with us kids playing on the prom or beach, Mum and Dad and Uncle Lawrence and Auntie Vera chatting in the deckchairs until it was suggested they adjourn to the pub for a quick wetting of the whistle, to wash away the sand. Everything was left on the beach, with a Grandma in charge as they wandered to the "Ship". We awaited their return eagerly as the promise of some crisps was usually kept, whooping around them on their return,

190

and looking for any sign of the promised crisps. Then the competition to find the little blue salt bag would be intense, as our appetites, whetted by the salt air, were satisfied.

Eventually all the paraphernalia was gathered up and the even longer trail off the beach began, with all the rugs, empty flasks and windbreaks carried on sand-encrusted legs up the little ravine and up the steps to the caravan site, where all thirsts were well satisfied by cups of tea.

Saltburn is still pretty much the same today. The caravan site is still there, although it has grown, and the football field where we ducked under the fence and played as children in the long summer grass is now part of it. The ravine is still the same, and the beach where we jumped over the breakers is now the haunt of surfers, clad in wet suits to keep out the chill of the sea. A recent visit brought alive many memories, and I walked the seemingly long trail down the little ravine in ten minutes. I climbed up the steps to the caravan site which I had last seen in the 1950s, and it all looked exactly the same, despite the football field being full of caravans and the grass short. I walked to where I thought the caravan had stood, and yes, the memories all came flooding back. As I stood deep in thought and reliving my childhood memories, I couldn't help but feel that, if Auntie Vera could stand beside me now, she wouldn't approve of the big grey substation that was buzzing furiously and sited exactly on the spot where her small caravan had once stood.

At times we met up with Auntie Phyllis nearby. As an enthusiastic amateur artist, her husband, Uncle Tom, spent most of his holidays in the nearby quaint old town of Whitby, painting the old yards and cottages and the glorious scenery around the North Yorkshire Moors. We loved Whitby too, but we only spent the odd holiday there, Mum and Dad preferring the west side of the country and "down South". The sea frets were a deterrent to Mum, but when they acquired a caravan in later years we had some nice holidays there. Staying at Saltwick Nab, on the very top of the cliff, when it was windy, the caravan would rock like fury and anything stored underneath the caravan was either missing or on the beach the next morning, including the odd tent that wasn't anchored down securely. When the sea fret rolled in and the fog signal started up, being less than half a mile away we didn't get much sleep, but it was a very spectacular setting. One year it was foggy all week, and we returned home early to get away from the fog signal and get a bit of sleep. Thankfully that fog signal has now been retired, and not before time.

Auntie Phyllis always stayed bed and board, in one of the little houses in the narrow back streets, taking food for the landlady to cook for them, which the landladies did in those days. When we went, we lived on fish and chips, and excellent they were, too. Morning, noon and night. When we came home we couldn't face them, but they were nothing like Whitby fish and chips in Bolton, for there was no fish there fresh out of the sea. Quite spoiled we were by Whitby fish and chips. We even went fishing with Dad on a sea fishing trip, to see if we could catch our own fish to take home, catching mackerel by the score. We couldn't pull them up fast enough, and they fell off the hook as they were lifted into the boat. The sea was quite rough too, but it was very enjoyable. Mum wasn't a sailor so she wouldn't go but watched for us on the pier, coming onto the pier extensions to see what we had caught.

When we were there, we always went to Scarborough too. That was where Mum picked up her fear of the sea. One day, Mum, Dad, Auntie Vera and Uncle Lawrence had hired a rowing boat and rowed out to sea. When they turned to come in, so had the tide, leaving them a very strong current to row against to come into the harbour. Mum thought their number was up, and, though they didn't panic, it took them ages to row back. Ever after Mum steered clear of boats, even on rivers. And she was a poor swimmer, unlike Dad who swam like a fish. Even after years of splashing about in the shallows and Dad's tuition, the fear of water was never overcome, and the sad tale of the Scarborough near-drowning was trotted out to us every time we were within five miles of the place.

Eventually the year moved on and all the holidays were over. It was the end of the six-week holidays, time to go back to school and move up a class with a new teacher in charge. Mum would have to buy us new winter clothes, our last year's well grown out of despite the six-inch hems. When we reached the age of eleven, there was to be a parting we hadn't anticipated, with one of us passing a scholarship and the other one not, something she had been quietly dreading.

CHAPTER
TEN

A Class Apart

Our last year in junior school was the build-up to the all-important school scholarship exam which dictated which school we attended from the age of eleven. It was usually taken at Bolton County Grammar School in Great Moor Street. Our teacher worked us very hard that year, with lots of maths and English tests in readiness for the real thing. Everything was done to prepare us and we were geared up with little pep talks on what to expect. The day duly arrived, and, despite the pep talks, we didn't really know what to expect but hoped for the best anyway. In a show of support Mum took us down and wished us luck as she gave our names to the severe-looking teacher in the school hall. After milling about for a bit in the general confusion, we were eventually siphoned off into a classroom to sit the exam. It was nerve-wrecking in as much as the classroom and school hall were strangely impersonal. Not at all like our junior school classrooms which had our paintings and poems decorating the walls. Everything was strictly done, with an air of importance.

We had three papers to sit; Maths, English and what was then known as a spatial test, better known now as an I.Q. test. Then, it was quite new. In the 1950s state schools were split into grammar schools, technical schools, and secondary moderns, where you went if you weren't clever enough to pass the scholarship exam. In our school, Sunning Hill, the top floor was occupied by the seniors, in other words those who had failed the school scholarship and just moved up, swapping classrooms every year in a progression round the seniors' hall until they were old enough to leave at fifteen and start work. If you passed for Grammar School, you were regarded as clever. Some of the top-notch swots, who were always top of the class, had a chance to sit the entrance exam for Bolton School. It was a chance for a private education as the school was fee-paying. Some fee-paid scholarships were awarded to give children with potential the chance to attend. It was only the clever children who sat the exam. The clever ones who passed also had to be clever at avoiding the double snob syndrome, where they were pig in the middle; clever but poor, and looked down on by the rich kids whose parents' money, rather than brains, had got them a place.

Kids were cruel even in my day, and the class system was in full throttle in the 1950s, even in a place like Bolton. Kids from the lower classes going to Bolton School were taunted by their previous friends, who felt they were now "above them", leaving them isolated with a foot in both camps and sometimes unacceptable to both. Grammar Schools taught Latin, French and German. "Techs" were more middle of the road, and taught the practical crafts of technical drawing, metalwork and woodwork for the boys, and needlework, cookery, and art for us girls. Some language was taught, but not Latin. Our school also had a pre-nursing course for the girls who wanted to be nurses and mothercraft for the older girls, sometimes needed sooner than expected. Not many girls went on to college. You had to be exceptional to do that. Those who did were known as blue stockings.

The first we knew about the results was when Mum dashed upstairs with an envelope after the postman had been. It said that I had passed and had a place reserved for me at Hayward Bilateral School. The letter went on to explain that the school had two "streams", one technical and one modern, a step up from the secondary modern syllabus. We would both be attending the same school, but in different classes. I suppose it was better than two different schools. We could go to school together and meet in the playground and go home together. Mum was delighted, and we all went up that same night to have a look round. There were three schools on one base, a new concept at the time. Each building was very modern and mostly glass. The Grammar School, the latest to be built on the base, was opening in September. The Bilateral School had been open a couple of years, and the Secondary Modern, the first to be built, was looking a bit worse for wear. Each school had a large gymnasium and there was a science block, used by all the schools, and a block that housed the workshops and needlecraft room.

As we peered through the window, Mum's face lit up at the sight of all the modern electric sewing machines, little knowing it was where we were both to suffer intense humiliation in later years. There was also a cookery block, complete with small well-equipped partitioned kitchens where Jean and I would whip up the disasters to take home to Mum and Dad in the great effort of learning how to cook. A further block, yet to be built, was earmarked to house administration and offices and, rumour had it, a swimming pool. The site was a rough muddy area, full of builders' rubble and deep puddles. These puddles were the nearest we got to a swimming pool. Five years later, when we went out to face the world, saturated with our acquired knowledge, the site remained the same. Built on a slope, the Grammar School occupied the highest level, then the Bilateral, then at the bottom of the site the Secondary Modern, thus setting the social structure of the base, with the Grammar School lording it over the rest.

Admittedly, while I was there, the Grammar School kids were always better behaved, and cleaner. Their spanking new uniforms and well-polished shoes seemed to stay cleaner longer, in direct contrast to the Secondary Modern kids, who didn't wear uniform at first. It was only later in an attempt to smarten us all up and bump up the reputation of the school that they were required to wear it, and then we all had to conform to strict uniform. Woe betide us if we were spotted by a teacher, going to or coming from school without school cap or beret. Mum took us to Shaw's in Great Moor Street to be kitted out at great expense, at the cheapest shop on the list. Having two to kit out wasn't cheap, but she did manage to get us each a school tunic, blouse and tie, and a fine knit burgundy cardigan to begin with. Later we were kitted out with a blazer with a school badge on the pocket that wouldn't have met Billy Pike's standards at all. The burgundy gaberdine mackintosh we were supposed to have, which would have put Frank Spencer's to shame, we did without, having to wait until Mum saved up again. So we started our new school with grey winter coats, bought at C&A the previous year, covering our proud new uniforms in all their glory.

After six weeks or so, I remember being pulled to one side by Mrs. Humphries, my new form teacher, who asked, "Where is your school mackintosh?" It was very embarrassing to tell her, "Mum is still saving up for them," as she had two to buy. Mum was livid when I told her, and dispatched me with a stiff note to the school to give to the offending teacher, dropping it on her desk and scarpering as quick as I could to escape any resulting fallout. No more was said, and we eventually got the macs, very long, very scratchy and very Frank Spencer. They lasted three years, worn with school scarf "college style", until the sleeves crept up towards the elbow and the tunic appeared lower than the hem. We only ever had one and finished up wearing the blazer with the sleeves pushed up to hide their shortness to come and go in. I remember standing at the bus stop in the bitter winter winds, dodging in and out of doorways to keep warm and looking for the bus coming up Derby Street, hoping it wasn't full, which it nearly always was, and flagging down the number 12 into Manchester, which left a walk of several blocks in the freezing winter weather. That year duffel coats came into fashion, and Mum bought us each one in burgundy. More and more kids turned up in them, and school gaberdine macs died a death as the duffel coat craze swept through school, much to the relief of the Mums and Dads, whose pockets were decidedly better off.

Only having one of everything caused something of a problem, for we had to see the week out in our school clothes. Mum washed what she could at the weekend in readiness for Monday, but often, especially in winter, only washed the cardigan, tunic and tie at half term as any shrinkage would mean she had to replace them, a costly expense with two of us. The wool in those days was prone to mill up and too much washing shortened its life span, especially in the little Hoover washing machine that knotted everything up. By the time half term was approaching, the woollen serge tunic was able to stand up on its own, and anything spilt down it tended to leave a clean patch, despite several quick spongings and pressings to merge the muck into one on Mum's rickety old ironing board.

After enduring five years of scratchy woollen serge, I can only say thank God for polyester and machine-washable wool. On a wet day the smell of damp woollen surge, tinged with Dad's Capstan Full Strength tobacco, combined with several bake house smells to make a concoction barely masking the smell of underlying dirt. Hanging in the air above my school desk, it all vied with the smell of Jeyes fluid liberally splashed about by over-enthusiastic school cleaners who firmly believed in overkill. To this day the pungent smell of Jeyes fluid brings back my schooldays, reminding me of the smell of my less than fresh school uniform on a damp day eagerly awaiting its half term wash.

When the spring term commenced at Easter, we were thrust, regardless of the weather, into cotton dresses. There we fared a little better. We each had two floral prints and one candy stripe, all pea green. But we had a change midweek because Mum made us two dresses of each, the material cut from two bolts of fabric bought from Shaw's. As the cotton was washed, it went limp and Mum had to starch it. Even so it creased and after a couple of days the white Peter Pan collars gathered the dirt from the atmosphere. But it was wonderful after the scratchy smelly serge of winter, worn through to half term and stiffening as it went.

Worn with blazer and beret, we actually looked quite smart and fresh in them and eagerly awaited the passing of Easter for our liberation from the school tunic. Being the 1950s, full skirts were all the fashion. Ours weren't, as Mum stinted on the material. Ours had short sleeves, Peter Pan collars, fitted waistlines, and unevenly gathered semi-full skirts, held out ballerina style by a paper nylon underskirt. Mum being Mum made ours out of a bit of paper nylon, again unevenly gathered into two tiers. And she stinted on us again by just making two tiers when everybody else had three. While they were new, the sharp edges on the seams made big red scratches on our legs, and when

200

they had been washed a time or two they clung limply to our legs despite the odd crack of static electricity that shot through them now and again. Sugar and water cured the limpness, but we couldn't do much about the static electricity, and as for the raw legs, well — as Mum was always saying when she permed our hair, "Pride's Painful". It was too, but Mum was always there with the Germolene and lots of sympathy. Still, we were "in fashion". Later she bought us net petticoats when the others had begun to fray along with Mum's patience for the sugar and water stiffening process. Pretty as they looked, sitting at a school desk proved to be a problem as the front's shot up and had to be wedged under the school desk when we sat down. We got fed up with them in the end and went without. Pride out of the window in favour of freedom.

The next fashion to hit school was ballerina shoes, black and with an elasticated heel to hold them on. We were the bee's knees that summer, but when autumn came, fallen arches, caused by the lack of proper support in the ballerina shoes, saw me in the doctor's waiting room. So much for ballerina shoes as that winter saw me doing exercises to lift up the arches.

We managed to make new friends in our individual classes and met in the playground to go home for our dinners, which Mum managed to scrape together in between serving in the shop. Homework was a big shock to our system, never having had any at junior school. Two hours was dished out each night. Half an hour for each subject was allotted, but, with four or more subjects and a floating essay to be in for a set date, it mounted up alarmingly. Especially maths, which now included the dreaded algebra and geometry for which I have never found any use whatsoever in my life after leaving school. Mum insisted we did it all as soon as we came in from school, leaving us free to play after tea. Begging a cake from what was left, we trundled begrudgingly upstairs to dash it off as quickly as possible, sitting on our beds. If it was history, then a visit to the reference library was often called for as we were set the task of researching a subject. How they must have groaned when they saw us coming. Enquiring at the desk, we were suitably fixed up with our research subject, and allowed to take the books up to the balcony on the first floor, which was divided into booths of sorts. Research done, in the relief the giggles took over. Loud giggles. The librarian was often hot-foot after us to keep down the noise which carried quite far in the silence. His face, puce with the effort of running up the stairs, often appeared around the bookcases and deepened in his fury. Well-chastised and threatened with being barred, we managed to keep down the noise, and stuck out our tongues as he disappeared downstairs again. But he was always helpful and got to know us, peering over his glasses as he handed us the required books, extracting a promise of good behaviour. Try as we would the giggles simmered to the surface as we tried to do our serious homework. His patience was unending; he was a real gem and never complained to school about us, despite the lip we occasionally gave him. He must have breathed a sigh of relief to see the back of us, though.

Teachers in our school were a different kettle of fish to our junior school teachers. Some ruled their class with a wooden cane of strict discipline. The boys especially were singled out, and punishment was meted out that wouldn't be tolerated in today's schools. A short smarting sharp rap on the back of the head with a ruler was enough to bring tears to the eyes and attention back to the subject in question. A mere whisper to a classmate would bring down a torrent of abuse and a "You, boy", as a board duster and a piece of chalk whistled in your direction without any hesitation. God help you if you dodged it too. One cheeky wit, braver than most, ducked to avoid one such missile with a quick quip of "Missed, Sir" and a smirk; only to be too slow to dodge the second, which caught him full on the side of the head. The teacher's return quip of "That didn't" wiped the smirk off the culprit's face pretty sharply, and made the rest of us pretty attentive to that teacher for a while. One poor soul was sent to the sick room with a badly cut head after a brush with a board duster. His parents must have been appalled, but, as was the custom of the time, it was assumed he had done something to deserve it. After a few questions all round, the matter was dropped and the fuss died down pretty quickly. Some of the boys did deserve it, though.

One of their tricks was bits of blotting paper well soaked in the inkwell, catapulted with a wooden ruler at unsuspecting targets from behind a desk lid. The resulting mess this caused led to the ending of the little pot inkwells in the school desks being filled with ink.

Any pupil possessing a bottle of Quink ink was pestered incessantly for refills of our newly acquired fountain pens. The more enterprising charged a penny a fill, or exacted a promise of a piece of a Wagon Wheel at break time. The fountain pens proved to be the perfect weapon for flicking ink at one and all.

Wet days saw the break times spent in the classroom as teachers took refuge in the staff room. Break over at the ringing of the school bells, a scout was sent out to warn of the teacher's approaching return and silence fell like a curtain again. The school scourge was a sweet-looking old lady, who taught needlework. Her schizophrenic outbursts became legendary as she whipped herself up to a crescendo at the sight of over-large tacking stitches. Her fury lasted unabated the full hour and a half of the double lesson as we cowered, not daring to scrape a chair which sent her over the edge completely. Never one to invite her wrath, I cowered the whole hour and a half behind the pretence of threading a needle, only to be sussed and pounced on as an example of sloth as she rent Mum's sewing homework apart and threw it on the floor while everyone gazed on in sympathy. Shaking like a leaf still, as the bell rang at the end of the lesson, I scraped my chair in the effort to escape quickly. Only to be pounced on once more, and given two hundred lines of "I must not scrape my chair", to be handed in at nine o'clock prompt the next day. The neatly written proffered lines were received with the grace of the Queen Mum. There was not a trace of the psychopath who had so terrorised me the previous day. Mum had to do the homework again, and was not best pleased that her efforts were so detrimentally treated. I was quaking as I awaited the verdict, but this time Mum had come up trumps. It passed inspection for stitching and I puffed up visibly with relief. Too soon, I might add, for the creased and rumpled mess brought about by my sweaty palms as I waited in line for the verdict on Mum's homework threw her into a frenzy, and I cowered once more as she hurled abuse and waved it around like a mad woman, finally pouncing on a fellow sufferer for sniggering.

We all suffered at her hands, and crept about on tiptoes from sewing desk to sewing machine. Any dropping of the scissors exacted a scream like a banshee and a glare from our classmates for "Setting her off". The worst experience was to be given the task of making a blouse. Mum chose the pattern, which proved to be beyond her sewing ability, possessing puff sleeves and a row of tiny button holes. Try as we might, she couldn't get it right and the wretched thing became the bane of our lives, both of us dreading the weekly sewing lesson. The puff sleeves I managed to make last for several lessons, with Mum gathering and resetting them over and over again in the effort to placate the harridan. One lesson, the horrible things were snatched from under my nose and taken to her desk to be reset expertly, to show us how it should be done. The next week however they were once again snatched and held up as I was made an example of for "bad tailoring" — the work done by her the previous week. The button holes I managed to stretch to the end of term, doing one a week, each being unpicked till the edges frayed. As was Mum's temper. After many attempts and the near loss of our sanity, we both managed to join in the throwing to the other side of the room of the dreadful thing though Mum's gathering improved somewhat, if not her temper. Next time we had to make something we chose a simple dirndl skirt from the "easy to make" range, and Mum decided on a cotton floral material that was easy to match, Mum's gathering by now being top class. We got as crafty as she was (pardon the pun) but, despite all the effort, Mum and I never came top of the class.

Eventually she was retired after one monumental outburst which saw her lose it completely. One enterprising girl, to whom we were all eternally grateful, went for the cookery mistress to witness her fury, fearing for her health as she rent the air with her fists, breathless, her face purple with rage at the minor misdemeanour of scraping a chair. She was lead off to a cup of tea and a chat with the headmaster, as we breathed a sigh of relief for the brief respite from her ranting and raving. She was right about the blouse, however. Even hovering on the edge, she had an eye for a bad fitting. It finished up in the bakehouse, used to wipe Dad's pie tins. All Mum's homework had been in vain.

Miss Hainey, our saviour, was a domestic science teacher, young and pretty in a matronly way. Her frequent and informal lessons were like a breath of fresh air after the horrors of the needlework room. She took us gaily through the mysteries of flaky pastry and soufflés in a concentrated effort to avert the gastric ulcers of our future families. Safe in her kindly care, we trooped into her culinary lessons with wicker baskets, a tea towel covering an ounce of this and that, to be put together in some culinary masterpiece and carted home on the bus after school. We waded through custard tarts, hoping ours would turn out like Miss Hainey's, fluffy and golden under a light dusting of nutmeg, to be taken from the oven and placed like hers proudly on the kitchen's formica table. Sadly it was never to be, as a mound of pastry rose like Vesuvius in the middle of a lump-laden mess. As daughters of a master baker, we hung our heads in shame and "jiggled" it on the bus home until it was unrecognisable for what it was, furtively relegating it to the dustbin before Dad could see it, with the excuse that it had been dropped on the bus home, and landed upside down. For that's just how it looked residing at the bottom of our dustbin when Dad managed a quick furtive peek in the back yard. The worst ever disaster was a toad-in-the-hole, which turned out of the oven rock solid in a futile attempt to crisp up the sausages. Miss Hainey's "Oh dear" was not much consolation as it was chipped out of the tin with the aid of a strong hand. Neither was the rest of the lesson, when I was given the task of trying to get the tin clean for some other poor unfortunate soul with the experience to come in the next lesson. My one real masterpiece was a lemon soufflé which didn't require any cooking at all. But, careful as I was with my masterpiece, even that didn't survive the bus journey home, when I had to stand up in a crowded school bus, carefully guarding the wicker basket as I moved shakily out of the way to let people off. Going straight in the bakehouse to reveal the magnificent masterpiece, I peeled off the tea towel to reveal a flattened battered mush which produced howls of laughter from Mum and Dad, who wouldn't believe how well it had turned out.

In one exam we cooked as a team, doing a three-course meal, ambitious to say the least, considering our expertise was sadly lacking, mine especially. Wisely, I was given the job of cooking the carrots and making tomato soup. The soup turned out OK, despite my melting the nylon sieve when I made the mistake of sieving it straight from the stove at simmering heat. The carrots, which seemed simple enough, were boiled for an hour, and might as well have been out of a tin as they tasted well stewed and salty despite watering them down well after I had forgotten them while I was dealing with the melted sieve and trying to hide it at the back of the cupboard. We had to eat the meal as well, and apart from the carrot's funny taste and the slight flavour of burnt nylon mesh in the tomato soup, it was OK. We managed to pass the exam too which was saying something, and we all managed to turn up to school the following day. No upset tums, which was surprising after the amount of burnt plastic we had all ingested. Perhaps the saturation of salt sterilised it all.

As culinary successes go, the triumph didn't last long and following successes were few and far between. Disaster followed disaster and it became a huge joke as it was all brought home in a sorry state. Sometimes it tasted better than it looked, but no-one was brave enough to take the risk, and it was mostly examined, laughed over, and promptly relegated to the bin on a weekly basis. The cookery lessons were looked forward to with glee as they afforded Mum and Dad a good laugh at our expense. The loser in all this, however, was Mum, because she had to stump up the cash for the ingredients. She must have breathed a sigh of relief when it was biscuits or a cake because she could raid Dad's bakehouse. This caused a few disasters in itself because his stuff wasn't labelled. I often ended up with the wrong things — salt instead of caster sugar, milk powder instead of cornflour spring painfully to mind. Miss Hainey always found me the right ingredients, so Mum's subterfuge, if it was that, came to no avail. One week, she mixed up the measurements of flour and sugar, and the light fluffy fairy cakes came out like granite tombstones, burnt nearly black on the edges with the middles sunk, all crumbling away and soft, because there was too much sugar and not enough flour. They tasted OK even if they had been in the oven an hour while I was trying to get the middles to set. All crunchy and sweet. Everybody had one; they went like hot cakes. Miss Hainey, lovely lady that she was, persevered, and I eventually turned out to be a reasonably good cook. I even managed to pass my G.C.E., quite an achievement after a disastrous beginning. But then I often wonder what I would have done without that bus home to blame it all on, and Mum's mixed-up ingredients.

Those first two years at secondary school were quite an eye opener. Apart from cookery and needlework, games (never a strong point for me) turned out to be a bit of a bind. Tossed out on to the school playing fields clad only in shorts and a cellular blouse in the depth of winter, the wind found its way to places I wasn't yet aware I had. I don't know why we were "volunteered" for lacrosse instead of hockey, but we were and found our heads and ears were targets instead of the usual shins and ankles. Mrs. Wilson, the games mistress, had cruelty engraved on her very soul, running us up and down the school playing fields with relentless cries of "Run, girls, run!" while she stood on the edges clad in a warm track suit. Later, when she was pregnant, a chair was added to the equipment. And she sat there, muffled up in coat and scarf, putting us through our paces. To add insult to injury we had to carry the chair out and back again. After we were coated in mud, and battered to death about the head and ears, it was back to the showers to thaw out. Clothes off in a unheated changing room and a run starkers through a line of showers squirting cold water. Shy at the best of times, embarrassed and self-conscious, the showers were a bigger ordeal than the games. There was nowhere to hide. The only way to lessen the ordeal was to get back first, and get it over with before Mrs. Wilson had gathered all the lacrosse sticks together. As soon as that whistle blew, I could step up speed to a warp nine in the effort to get back to the changing room before her. The only trouble was everyone else had the same idea. Including Mrs. Wilson.

I hated games, and it showed as I hovered on the periphery of every game, reluctance written all over my face, and convinced my legs weren't made for running. To make matters worse, I was always the last to be picked to be included in a team. That's where my efforts really paid off, as I stood at the back dodging out of sight. As the numbers dwindled the unlucky team captain had no option but to include me, and as I was always the very last to be picked, it now and then occurred to me that I might be unpopular. But what the hell. I hated Mrs Wilson's beady little eyes as they followed us through the changing room. It was with glee that she made us dash through that line of freezing cold showers, searching for any excuse to send us through again. When one girl slipped, the pile up was spectacular, and Mrs. Wilson had to turn off the showers to sort us all out, not wanting to get wet herself and suffer the experience she put us regularly through. The girls whose periods had started were excused that week, but had to bring a note from their mothers. It was with a certain one upmanship they waved the valuable things in front of our noses. We wished ours would start so we could get an "excused showers" once a month. Rounders was the only game I enjoyed, but even that wasn't played in the normal way, like in the mill yard. The bats were circular, not flat which gave a good broad surface to hit the ball. These bats were not much thicker than a broom handle, and the ball was hard leather like a cricket ball so I stood hardly a chance of getting ball to bat, and was usually out first ball when my legs refused to carry me to the first base

211

before the ball was thrown to the first base keeper and touched to the base pole before I did. When out, I stood shivering on the sidelines, watching the more athletic notch up the runs and dreading the fielding to come. That little ball was responsible for some massive bruises, and even if we pulled our hands back to cushion the blow, it stung something rotten, leaving no alternative but to grin and bear it or drop the wretched thing and risk the ire of the rest of the team who actually took the game seriously. Once I actually made a good effort and managed to be the last one left in to bat. Having the best of three to go at, I managed to bounce a limp second ball into the boundary in my panic, but not far enough to get round on my run-out legs. I was rounded on squarely by the rest of the team and sent to Coventry for the rest of the day for not waiting to bat the third ball which I might have hit further.

P.T. was even worse. We were put through the exercises on horse and beam and floor. Here Mrs Wilson really came into her own and we were crucified by having to hang from ropes and climb bars in the name of vigorous exercise. The day after it was difficult to walk as the stretched muscles stiffened up and my pelvic floor set rock solid. To make it worse we had to wear navy blue knickers that showed any wet patch of perspiration as a weak bladder, causing endless embarrassment, and all efforts to check were seen as groping oneself. The only way to make sure was to line the crotch with toilet paper in the changing room. It lasted for a while but in the strenuous exercise became either soggy or dislodged itself, leading to nudges and winks from fellow sufferers in the floor exercises. Eventually it would be discreetly removed in a quiet moment or in the middle of a crowd and pushed up a sleeve, where it finally managed to end up on the gymnasium floor, and remain in full view, all soggy and screwed up and glaringly white.

Mum had no sympathy and I suffered agonies in gym class. When our periods started, she made us wear sanitary towels, and not Tampax like other girls did in the gym, deeming it "not proper" for girls of our age to wear internal sanitary protection. So the exercises were done with a big wedge of sanitary towel in our gym knickers, causing endless embarrassment but cushioning the hardness of the floor. Try as I might my legs never did manage to get into running gear, and school sports day often proved to be a problem. One year I was "elected" to run in the relay team for my school house, Livingstone. We had to earn points for the house in the track and field competitions, and everyone was dragged on to the playing fields on the fateful day and draped with a coloured band of the house colours diagonally across the chest. Despite my best efforts, I managed to earn no points at all, crashing out of the race with legs asunder in full view of Mrs. Wilson and my house captain to my great shame. I did my best not to cause a fuss, slinking away in the embarrassment of it all, receiving no sympathy despite the fact that I had hurt myself. The rest of the competition was spent in the toilets trying to relocate my legs into their sockets and get the wobbly things back into working order.

The nightmare never ended. When we played netball in winter, being tall for my age I was always called upon to play goal defence. As games went this was my best effort. In the cut and thrust of the game, I was restricted to the home side of the court. The ball had to come to me. Despite the odd tussle with the rough goal attack, when I was likely to receive an elbow or two in my face, the games were quite boring, so I was left to watch most of the game without ever really taking part. I reckoned I'd cracked it. The last year at school found me in the toilets with the rest of the games dodgers, swapping gossip. Even this I wasn't good at, and I began to think the games periods were cursed. My shyness with other girls severely limited my ability to have a good bitch, although I reluctantly joined in listening to the sex talk, and of who was getting it from whom.

By this time Mrs. Wilson had gone. Married and up the spout to a fellow teacher, who also had a knack of making his pupils squirm by the over-enthusiastic use of the cane. They were made for each other. Our new teacher was younger and more flexible, but games still had no appeal and I dreaded them. I made a conscious effort to forget my kit, racking up loads of detention in the process. Still, it was the lesser of the two evils, and the half hour gave me the chance to do some of my homework in peace. Occasionally the odd sadistic teacher was in charge, who thought it funny for us to spend some of the time with our hands on our head, but detention was usually done on a rota, and some of the teachers thought it wise to use the time to get some marking done, leaving us to do our homework quietly in the process.

The maths homework caused us some problems, and Dad's algebra was sadly not up to scratch. We spent hours trying to get a grip on the senseless problems in the first two years. We often gave up and I came clean at school the next day, admitting to not having a clue, despite the lesson. The problems set for homework never seem to match up with the lesson, and the value of x, y and z remained unattainable to me and Dad. Give Dad his due he did try, and must have been extremely relieved when we dropped the subject after the second year. Mum was the one to help with the English. She once polished off an essay on "My Ideal Home" in no time at all when I was overloaded with homework one weekend. Got a nine for it too, which is more than Dad ever got for his algebra despite his grammar school education. I usually enjoyed the English lessons, and we read aloud in class some cracking books, leaving me to extend my reading away from the Enid Blyton range. The one thing I hated was poetry, and learning a poem and reciting it in class was something to be dreaded, standing there at the front of the class squirming, stammering, face bright red, trying to remember the wretched thing and give it some meaning. Of course I always fluffed it; funnily enough the person before and after me always was word perfect. Wouldn't you know it. I would sit shaking till the end of the lesson, trying to hide my red flush by sinking my neck as far into the collar of my blouse as far as it would go. Of course I was always pounced on to answer a question just as the flush was dying down, and all eyes turned in my direction once more, wondering if I was struck down by a sudden deformity because my head started straight from my chest. It's awful to be shy, but I must say I was never bullied, and every effort was made to draw me "out" though this was an embarrassment in itself as I was picked on to stand up and be brought forth.

CHAPTER
ELEVEN

Teen Years

After two years at Hayward Bilateral School, Jean and I were verging on our teenage years. My special friend Lois, to whom I had stuck like glue in the hope that some of her natural confidence would rub off on me, was suddenly separated from me as we were put into different classes. Lois was altogether brighter than me, and an only child. We would meet on Saturdays to go into town and look at the shops, pointing out all the things we would buy if only our Mums would give us the money. The fact that our Mums didn't have the money was a bone of contention. Lois's Mum worked full time in the mill, leaving her to see to herself much of the time. Accordingly she had to help with the housework. Her Dad was a real stinker at times; very strict, keeping a tight control on her, especially where boys were concerned. She always called him Daddy. He always had the last word, and would often be in a strop when we called for her to go out. Sometimes he wouldn't let her out, despite the pleas and promises, and we had to leave her tearful at the front door, grounded. As we reached puberty, there was a definite difference between Jean and me and Lois. Even though we were almost the same age, Lois blossomed and attracted lads like wasps to a jam jar. She developed well-upholstered curves in all the right places and had a fully developed chest complete with brassiere while ours stayed flat under Mum's ever insistent liberty bodice and vest. I often think our lack of development in that area was down to the constraint of our tightening liberty bodice. Much as I loved twiddling with the sticky and bendy rubber buttons, that slowly perished in the wash, through my school blouse, I would have given anything for a bosom and a pretty lace brassiere just like Lois's. The flat chest was becoming more and more of an embarrassment in the games changing room as I followed one bouncy chest after another in the quick dash through the showers. Most of my class had started their periods too, proudly brandishing notes from their Mums to excuse them from showers after games, something I would have cheerfully killed for.

Subtle changes were noticed, however, that showed something was on the way. Spots started to appear on our foreheads, beginning their ever-downward journey to our noses and chins. Our hair, never one of our best features, fine and flyaway at best or permed to tight frizz in Mum's amateur hairdressing ventures, developed an oil slick of its own, became lank and stuck to our scalps, adding its own aroma to the smelly bake-house/Capstan Full Strength halo hovering above our school desks. Above all Lois developed slight B.O. and as we sat together everyone assumed it was me. Between us we smelled like a greasy spoon transport caff, and, as Lois was better turned out, I took the blame, and willingly so, never saying boo to a goose, as was my way. To record all this horror, the school photographer turned up at regular intervals and we were dished out the fruits of his labour to be taken home to Mum and Dad. Far from being delighted, they dispatched them back to school promptly the next day, after much merriment. It was embarrassing to say the least, returning them when Dad had coated them in flour, but we were glad to get rid of the horrors, especially before Mum had a chance to show them in the shop to all the customers as a form of in-house entertainment.

The one thing that did develop was our feet which grew at an alarming rate. Mum insisted in hiding them in clumpy shoes, with lace ups too, which made our legs look even more stick like. In summer it was still the Clarks T-bar sandals, which slid out of shape far too quickly, or the crippling ballerinas with the elastic that dug ruts in the back of our heels. In any event, viewed side on we looked like a capital letter L. In contrast to all this, Lois, with her usual contingency of admirers following in her wake, developed a sexy little wiggle, and her fresh complexion, sweet-smelling hair and hour-glass figure were reflected in the girls' toilet mirror at the side of mine. Soul-destroying to say the least. Far from hating her reflection, as I did, it became her constant companion as she patted and preened in deep satisfaction, dashing to the toilets at every opportunity and spending the break time there. Her tiny waist complemented the ever-growing bosom in the pretty organza dresses made by her Mum. In tight waists and V-necked "Marilyn Monroe" bodices with full flowing skirts, perfectly gathered, her neat figure pranced daintily at the side of mine, flat-chested and big footed. I attempted to stem the oil slick that had assailed me with useless products bought by Mum in an attempt to stop the spots. It was all to no avail. To top it all, the longed-for periods had arrived at last, which sent Mum scurrying down to Mr. Costello's for two packets of Dr. Whites. Appalled at the mess, and horrified at the pain, our first instinct was to send them back. Mum sympathised lovingly and came up with two Aspirin and a cup of hot milk to ease the cramps.

There was no pep talk on the virtues of the woman's body, not that we expected one, but the promise of a note to "excuse showers" brightened us up no end. Still, it wasn't much to look forward to every month, despite the precious note. Mum, still tuned to the old wives' tales, wouldn't let us wash our hair in case we died, so we had to endure the greasy hair as well. And a ban was imposed on the swimming baths, because Tampax, which most of our friends used, was deemed improper to "Girls like us". Not to mention being embarrassed in front of Dad, when her eyebrows shot up at the mention of it. It was an absolutely awful time. When we were all "on", the scramble for Dr. Whites became manic. There was never enough to go round and I used to hide the last one so I didn't have to be the one to "nip down to Mr. Costello's" with two shillings for another packet, which was such an ordeal because he never wrapped them up. Mum would hide them

220

under her coat and we were given instructions to do the same, and not shame the family by being seen with them. It was all right in winter, but in summer it looked ridiculous as we scurried furtively back with a big lump under our winter coats on a gloriously hot day.

Poor Mr. Costello, he was even more embarrassed than us. We embarrassed one another by the fact that we were embarrassed, as we emerged as pink from his shop and as hot under the collar as him. Poor man, it was certainly different to buying the two ounces of sweets in a cornet bag he had doled out with the dewdrop hanging off the end of his nose, and of the partaking of a glass of his weak Vimto on the bench at the side of the shop. If there was anyone in the shop, we would wait until they had gone, hanging about on the step till the shop had emptied.

There was a certain difference in the way we carried our satchels too. Instead of slung over our shoulder, they now had to be tucked under the right arm, resting on the hip, like the other girls did. For us it was a godsend, as the left arm could be draped across to hold it in place, thus disguising our flat chests. We left out the wiggle of the hips, though; on us it looked ridiculous. Eventually we started to "bud up", but it was a slow and painful process and Mum was reluctant to buy us a bra each. Finally she gave in and hurried us in to Marks and Spencer on a Saturday afternoon to buy us one each. They had to be washed and dried draped on the pipes in the airing cupboard overnight as necessary. They were white cotton, which yellowed in no time at all in the airing cupboard. Beehive shaped with circular stitching around the cups, which made them stick out in two sharp points, they soon crumpled inwards as there wasn't much to keep them from collapsing at first. So we stuffed them with toilet roll, which wasn't much fun as it was the hard shiny kind that smelled of disinfectant. When we discovered padded bras, we pestered her to death until she bought us one. We must have been fifteen then, so it was quite a time to hide the grotty ones in the changing room at games. I don't know what Jean did, but I stuffed mine in my shoes.

Our excursions into the wide world became more adventurous, too, as Jean and I and Lois became the intrepid three. Unlike us, Lois glowed with confidence, and we could only stand back and admire as she pelted her fists at lads who ventured a cheeky remark or two at her attributes. Trips to High Street Baths became exciting as she fought them off. One poor soul, his testosterone out of control, was driven to an attempted grope of her underwater and very nearly drowned in the process. He was fished out by the pool attendant and barred for a week, as she whispered coyly in the attendant's ear what he had done. Stamping on cockroaches became quite tame in comparison as the main preoccupation became Lois's paramours, who pestered us silly to give her messages and fix up a date. Through it all she patted and preened, Mum even turning the mirror to the wall when she appeared as she did often in the school holidays. She thought our shop was lovely and pestered Mum to let her serve. Not us. We disappeared like jack rabbits when a customer appeared, remembering the school photos and resisting the attempt to be dragged in. Mum took advantage of Lois now and again and disappeared into town for a good shop, leaving us all in charge. Lois served, overwhelmed with the thrill of it all, and begging to do it again the following week. It was all quite boring to us as it was usually slack in the afternoon, but Dad kept an eye on things.

Afternoons spent at Lois's house were more fun, as she was on her own and we had the house to ourselves. We played her record player and she dug out her Mum's love letters sent by her Dad during the war. Tied up with ribbon, they were trotted out on a regular basis to be examined closely for any cheeky talk, put carefully back in the drawer before her Mum came home. One afternoon we made skating skirts out of taffeta, decorating them with ric-rac braid. Cut out by her Mum, who measured our waists, we took turns on the treadle sewing machine under her supervision. An improvement on the wretched blouse, they were quite a success and greatly admired on our next trip to the skating rink, our Saturday afternoon treat. A lot of our time was spent in Woolworths, hanging around the cosmetic counter, which Lois liked to do. We tried all the lipsticks on the backs of our hands and dabbed Cream Puff powder on our shiny noses, discreetly, of course, as the counter staff, deep in their chatter, hovered at the other end of the counter. We could have helped ourselves to anything, they wouldn't have noticed. But after the incident of the little tomato in Bolton Market, when Mum's wrath descended on me after I "tried one", it wasn't a good idea. It didn't stop us from helping ourselves to the dabs of Evening in Paris, though, or the Californian Poppy, which were laid out as samples on the counter. Or the finger dips into the pots of Ponds Cold Cream, which wasn't cold, or the Vanishing Cream, which didn't make our spots vanish. We tried it all as the girls carried on with their conversation. If we wanted to buy anything, a brisk "Excuse me" was called for, also ignored until you became insistent. Then the offending article was haughtily snatched with a tut, and the shakily offered money banged into the till. A brown paper bag was snatched from under the counter in a huff, the article jammed into it and the lot thrown back at you along with any change due before they dashed back to catch up on any missed titbit of gossip or sniping that made up the main business of the day.

There must have been quite a bit of theft in the desperation to get served, because glass soon appeared over the goods and it wasn't half as much fun because we couldn't get at the stuff, and had to ask the girls. Getting them to notice us could take all day. They weren't very gracious either. About this time, I became even more unattractive beside Lois because I had to start wearing glasses. Another blow to my ego. The problem was spotted at school by the school doctor, who came now and again to examine us. Our chests were listened to before he peered down our throats, and our ears tested before the all-important eye test. I knew mine were bad when I couldn't read the blackboard in science. But then again, so were Lois's. We took turns going down to the front of the class on some excuse or other when we had anything to copy up. Our science teacher must have thought we had St Vitus Dance because we were always dashing down to sharpen a pencil over the waste basket or finding some excuse to get nearer to the board, to fathom out something we couldn't see clearly enough to read. Neither owned up to being unable to see. Both of us were adamant we wouldn't wear glasses. Despite desperate attempts to learn the eye chart furtively as we gave our details to the school nurse and waited in line, I managed to fluff it in the nerves of the moment and I was sussed. Unlike Lois, whose memory served her better and who sailed through the test.

An appointment was made at Flash Street Clinic, where they extracted teeth and did eye examinations. It was also a school for children with learning difficulties at one time, notorious and grim. It was where you went if something was the matter with you, so it was avoided like the plague. We had been on several occasions to have our bad teeth extracted by gas, an experience not to be recommended to the fainthearted, after which Mum would wrap a scarf around our mouth, with the regulation bloody handkerchief stuffed into it, and cart us groggily home to be sick, the after-effects of extreme fear, severe shock, and the gas. It was not without trepidation that we entered the dreadful place as it was a place of previous suffering remembered well from the milk teeth days. After my eyes were dilated by a man brandishing a giant syringe, I had to sit glassy-eyed in line, waiting for him to return. Mum kept looking at me

225

oddly. My pupils had dilated to the extent of having no irises, making me look like one of the undead. (Of course, tactless as ever, she didn't hesitate to tell me so, or Dad when we got home. Once more I was the butt of their jokes.) When he came back after what seemed like hours and ushered us into the small consulting room, a lazy eye was detected. In those days, this usually meant the good eye was blacked out to make the other one work, which sent me into a panic attack at the thought of it all. I could imagine myself now at the side of Lois, partially blinded, spotty and flat-chested. My spirits floored, I sat on the hard school chairs waiting in line again, to be blinded in one eye. Relief came in the form of a lovely lady in white who appeared like my guardian angel, brandishing a chit to take to the optician's for a pair of National Health spectacles. Horror struck once again; visualising Graham's elastoplast-enhanced National Health issue specs, I burst into floods of tears. I was hustled out by Mum and chastised for "showing her up". I blubbed all the way home, swearing adamantly I wouldn't wear them and begging to go private. If any money changed hands, I didn't see it, but I was fitted with a pair of pretty blue spectacles which looked better off than on. Badly fitting, they took up residence on a slippery area of my greasy nose and were on a perpetual downward movement, which had to be readjusted regularly. Lois was delighted, as the to-ing and fro-ing to the front of the science class ceased, and she just looked at my class exercise book instead. It was notable that her next best friend after we were split up into different classes at the end of the year also wore glasses, so delaying her need for a pair until she was nearly sixteen.

I hated mine. Always on a downward slide because of the oil slick on my nose, they needed perpetual pushings up. No matter how high I pushed them, their downward journey irritated and aggravated me to a point that they disappeared into my school satchel at the ringing of the school bell, leaving me to grope my blurred way into the school yard where everything merged into a distant haze. Before I started to wear them, despite the science blackboard, I didn't think I was blind at all. Admittedly I couldn't see the number on the school bus while it was in Great Moor Street and had to leave it till the last minute before leaping out to flag it down, often causing the driver to do a full emergency stop, at his discretion, leaving us to jog up Derby Street to get on well past the bus stop as he cursed and mopped his brow. It was one more nail in the coffin. Boys didn't make passes at girls who wore glasses, and to my dismay I was given the nickname "Speccy Four Eyes". None of it did anything for my shyness, and, instead of developing a "persona" like Lois, I slipped into invisibility beside her, her personality, confidence and voluptuous figure obliterating mine. Unattractive, and unsure of myself, I became boring and slipped into silence, no longer able to make the effort to compete with her.

Salvation came to a certain extent when we were separated. Put into different classes, I made new friends. This time once bitten twice shy, I joined a group of girls with whom I made up a foursome. None of us was stunning looking in the way Lois was, and two of us had spots, so I didn't have to suffer in isolation. Also, two of us wore specs and none of us had a wake of boys in tow, either, which made life a lot easier. I didn't have to suffer the indignity of the "Speccy Four Eyes" taunt on my own either, with Lois simpering on the sidelines and gloating over her lack of specs. Jean fared better than me as she was still with our junior school friends. Only one of these had bloomed, but not to the extent that Lois had.

Lois palled up with a girl of similar virtues and they competed to have the smallest waistlines, squashing themselves in with the strongest of "waspies", the popular belts of the time. I must admit to having a sneaking delight when Julia managed to outdo her on the figure stakes. Despite having spots and specs, she managed to out-sex her too at times with a sexy way of holding her school satchel, a slinky walk and a deep sexy voice. Obviously they were well on their way to become the school sirens. Funnily enough, they were ridiculed at the drop of a hat by most of the other girls. Not to their faces of course, and certainly not by girls like us, who were undeveloped and spotty, and not in the same class. Once parted, we continued to see each other at times, but Julia's pursuits (boys) were more exciting than ours. And we still played in the back street, when homework allowed, with boys, not at boys. We were still little girls, despite our budding up, and Mum dressed us as such if she could get away with it. The friendship eventually cooled off. Much to the relief of Mum, who said Lois was fast and that she was sick of turning the mirror to the wall when she came.

Life went on, however, and we continued to go to Granny's in the long summer holidays. She was getting older now, being well into her seventies. We only went for a week after Mum decided she was "failing", whatever that meant. Granted she had become a bit stooped and joked as we compared out heights, "You shooting up and me going back down." She was still the same, though, with the same hearty laugh and crinkly eyes, even if she couldn't keep up with us as well as she used to. What's more, we didn't both fit in the tin bath any more. Baths were taken in the kitchen now and not in front of the living room fire, because it wasn't as far to haul the water from the gas geyser. But we still shared the same bath water, helping to empty it with the big jug when we had done, and putting back the tin bath on the hook on the cellar wall where it was kept. She never ever acquired a washing machine, or any other mod cons, like a bathroom or indoor toilet. We still "went" in the yard, in the shared toilet, with the toilet paper being shared by the two houses. At least it was proper toilet paper now; we didn't have to cut up newspaper anymore, even though it was somewhat rationed. The washing was still done in the dolly tub, possed, wrung and rinsed, rinsed again and hung to dry in the back street on Mondays as usual. The rows with the coalman still went on too. He still hadn't learned and was regularly on Mondays chased from the entrance to the back street. Our Horsforth friends were growing up as well. At fifteen Brenda was about to

229

leave school; you did then. She had a boyfriend, too, and was to marry at sixteen. We never saw her again after that, although Granny kept the news of her up to date in her letters to Mum. We still shared the same bed, with the bolster down the middle. We were taking up more room now so it was a bit of a squash. We last went to stay when we were fourteen. Granny would have understood that as we grew up we would grow away from her, as all children do. She still came over to Bolton, and we loved having her, as we always did, going with Dad to meet her off the bus in Rochdale, with her small suitcase. She still came for Christmas and Easter to help out and the holidays in summer in caravans in Wales.

Despite her age she still rolled up her sleeves to do Mum's spring cleaning, pulling down the curtains right round the house. Occasionally she would disappear into town to look at the shops and Bolton Market, dodging the traffic nervously because she wasn't used to it. When she was coming, the bedstead would go up in our room and the senna pod glass dug out of the kitchenette for the nightly ritual. By this time we had acquired an old Dansette record player. Bought second-hand, of course. Rock and roll was just coming out, and all the girls at school were learning to "bop", something we found difficult to get the hang of, having two big left feet. We joined in the fashions, though, and Mum bought us two rock and roll skirts and trews to wear with our duffel coats.

Despite the Dancette and the fashion fads, we were still out of the flow because we didn't have a television set. Mum and Dad didn't want one, still going to the pictures regularly and reading and listening to the wireless after tea when the shop had closed. Dad was still tinkering with his cars in the back street on a regular basis, not yet having a posh one that was reliable. Only when we left school did he acquire the Sunbeam Talbot that was to put him in the same bracket as Billy Pike. Eventually, when we were approaching fifteen, the value of television did come home to Mum when we were asked to baby sit for the new couple next door in the old tripe shop. We were all hooked in no time at all, and they gave in "for our benefit", or so they said. Several Saturdays when we weren't asked in saw us sitting, staring at the wall, and missing it madly. They were hooked just as much as we were, and one suddenly appeared as a surprise for us. Second-hand of course, and hired from Edwin P. Lees, where it had been sent back for failure to pay the never never. It was scratched but we didn't mind. It was a telly, and it was installed in our living room, in the corner, where it stayed until the tube blew up two years later.

It quite changed our lives, opening our eyes to the world, and it was here to stay. We became avid television watchers, Mum and Dad too. It was switched on every night, but not till the homework was done and Mum had shut the shop. With a bag of sweets to pass round, there were never any arguments about what we would watch, because the programme was limited to the B.B.C. until I.T.V. started up. However, it livened up the winter nights and, like everyone else, we cut down on our visits to the pictures. The cinemas started to close down at an alarming rate, and soon the Majestic, the Ritz, and the Windsor all disappeared. The Tivoli, our Saturday matinee favourite, went over to Bingo and got far more queues than the pictures ever did, with hoards of women queuing down the side of Thomas Street. Mum never went, although some of our customers did. Dad was very derisory, calling it housey housey, a game he played at Auntie Vera's that he couldn't stand but played anyway. Coffee bars started up too, and we all became Americanised, drinking Espresso, which was then more froth than coffee, but very trendy. We called it froffy coffee, and drank it out of glass cups and saucers. We weren't old enough to go into pubs, and we didn't look eighteen like some of our classmates. With a lot of makeup and stiletto heels, they passed easily for eighteen, which gave them entry into the town centre pubs on the hunt for older boys to flirt with. Mum would have killed us if we did it, and called us "common" which was her ultimate insult in those days. Everyone who wore thick panstick makeup was common to Mum, tacking a "you could scrape it off" on the end. Especially if their skirt was tight and heels above two inches, the ladylike height. She didn't mind us going to the CasaBlanca, though, to sit on the tall stools drinking froffy coffee. The CasaBlanca was a popular meeting place for us and a lot of our schoolfriends in the late 1950s. Spanish in style with white stucco walls and lots of dark wood, it was owned by Pedro, a Bolton Spaniard, who later opened a wine bar. He was a man of vision because at the time places like these in Bolton were few and far between. We loved the laid-back atmosphere and the dark corners, especially the front room where we could perch on the tall stools, froffy coffee on the dark wood shelf that went round the room. We spent hours there, gossiping about teachers and prefects and discussing the latest records from Elvis. We were all smitten.

At school, the prefects were a rotten lot, even though they were the school elite. They oversaw movements about school, and were stationed at intervals on the staircases, ready to pounce on any misbehaviour. Between lessons, the whole school was on the move at once so it gave them the perfect opportunity to bully in the chaos, swooping here and there to take names and pushing the poor victim back into line. They were very uppity, with a sense of self-importance, and most of them were well-hated. Any small misdemeanour gave them the perfect opportunity to flex their minor authority, picking at will on the weakest. None of our circle were ever to make prefect, thankfully. But we were picked on many times, pulled out of line and kept to one side, making us late for lessons. They knew we would be, and that the wrath of the teacher would descend on us, thanks to them. They may have been outstanding pupils, but they had a lot to learn in social skills.

We had one school trip in my school years. That was a field trip to Southport, to study the life on the seashore. It was no strange place to us. We went there a lot with Mum and Dad, taking the car on to the beach, which was very wide. Dad would sometimes let us drive on the beach, along with Mum who wanted to learn but never quite had the confidence. We once got stuck in the soft sand with the tide coming in, slowly creeping around us as we were pulled out by a tractor. Dad wasn't worried, and kept his cool. Mum was pretty upset, thinking we were all going to drown and the car would be washed away. That put her off altogether, and she never did learn in the end, but we all had a few practices. It was great fun. The field trip was a bit of a disaster, too. We had to walk out to the sea to collect specimens, a journey of quite some distance. We all sat shattered, teachers too, in the sand hills when we got back, feet weary with the long walk. All clad in identical school macs, we ate our packed lunches in the shelter of the sand hills and, because it was windy, the sand got into all the food. It was quite an adventure at the time, for we hardly ever had school trips. Still we all enjoyed it, but we never went on any more.

Lots of girls started going to Bolton Palais, so they could meet Teddy boys. With some of them the attraction was their fashions and daring exploits. Or so they seemed on those days. We used to listen to them talking about them in their dinner hour. It was always about who fancied who, who necked with who and how far they had gone. One week there was a lot of excitement when there had been a fight in the ballroom. The talk went on for weeks, and we began to wonder if we were missing out on something. Our social occasions usually took in the monthly social dances at the Congregational Sunday School hall on Daubhill. They were hardly rave-ups, most of the ravers being over sixty and well into intricacies of Old Time and Square Dancing. We could manage to do quite a few as well, what with Granny's tuition and Mum and Dad's excursions to the Co-op Hall one winter before we got a telly. Mum bought us all some dancing shoes, such was the enthusiasm for a time, and Dad had Fred Astaire shiny patent leather, hoping Fred's expertise would rub off on him. Mum said he always danced with his bottom out. He did too, and looked painfully embarrassed, when Mum twirled like Ginger Rogers into the bandstand, knocking all the music stands over. Oh dear, parents.

We had got to that stage when the embarrassment they caused us led to some criticism. It all came to naught when they got tangled up in a Burns Night supper. The Gay Gordons done in kilts proved too much for Dad and led to some surreptitious sniggering. When the Haggis was piped into the supper room, we all neglected to stand up and were branded as Sassenachs. It was declared too posh, and the shoes remained in the bottom of the wardrobe, ours grown out of quickly and Mum's worn at the barracks dances. Dad's eventually were worn out in the bakehouse, the shiny patent dulled with a coat of flour.

As the Sunday School dances went, they were O.K. We all got up to do the Paul Jones, as it was a chance to dance with a man, even if they were all old. They made a fuss of us too, getting us up to do dances we couldn't do and sitting down when they could no longer tolerate our stepping on their toes. There was always a bit of a supper, usually potato pie, which was cheap to make and warmed us up in the freezing room. It finished about ten o'clock, when we were all thrown out by the caretaker, one of our friends' Dad, who wanted to lock up. Social life in this stage of our life was sometimes hectic because we attended all the Sunday School concerts there too, and the local operatic effort which was occasionally given in Peace Street Mission. They were all good dos, with a cup of tea at the interval and occasionally, depending on the state of the finances, a biscuit thrown in for free. There weren't always enough to go round, so the ones that got there first had first choice. Not that it mattered, because by the time you got back to your seat in the stampede it was soggy anyway from all the slopped tea in the saucer. Mum used to get the tickets in the shop in return for putting up a poster.

We got free tickets for the circus too, the advance booking office people coming round the week before and asking Mum to put up a poster. The circus was on Spa Road on the edge of Queens Park, where they moved in lock, stock and barrel after a big parade through the town. We always went down to see all the animals, some of which were in a pretty bad state. The horses were always OK, it was the lions usually that were a bit moth eaten. They kept them in big cages with wheels on. We could hear them growling sometimes when the wind was in the right direction. The seats were always badly put together, and the draught under the canvas tent was worse than in our living room. Like the fair people, they used to come in the shop. You could smell the animals on them; like old donkeys they smelled, and once the glamour of the circus makeup disappeared, they were very ordinary. When we were young we always went, but when we got older Mum would give the tickets away. They were always cheap tickets anyway. It was fun to hang around to see what was going on and if they treated the animals all right. It was just a shame to see them in cages all the time.

By now we were half children, half adult. It was strange not being one or the other. Like hanging on to one life yet wanting another. We were pretty late developers as children go nowadays, still playing out in the back street at times and yet craving to go out with boys while still being too shy to do so. No-one fancied us anyway. The shyness and the spots saw them off, so we hung about as all teenagers do, the erratic mood swings coming and going like the tides. Grandma Toothill came occasionally. But she seemed to get on Mum's nerves, especially with the loud shouts of "SHOP", sitting in the chair all day and making no effort to help. Poor Dad was in the middle, but he had nothing much to say. Any conversation seemed to be about years ago, when Dad and Auntie Vera were young. Mum's eyes would go up frequently to us and we were all glad when she went home, despite the odd flash of her dry humour. Like Granny she made a beeline for the market and had trouble finding her way back to the shop, loaded up with cheap cotton to knit into endless dishcloths. She sat so long she tottered when she got up, diving off into the fireplace recess on occasions before she gained her equilibrium and tottered back. Sometimes she couldn't put up with our noise, and we were shushed so she could listen in on the conversation going on in the shop. It caused endless rows between Mum and Dad as she went behind each of their backs to rat on some of the things she'd overheard in the shop. In the end we'd groan when she was coming, because then we had to sleep in Mum and Dad's room and there was no privacy for any of us. Poor Grandma, she never meant to be any trouble; it just turned out that way.

I don't know if she enjoyed the visit. She brightened visibly when it was time to take her home, packing the crocheting threads and the Buttercup syrup away gleefully into her suitcase, along with the giant pink bloomers that had hogged our clothes line in relays all week. I think we made more of a fuss of her when she was leaving than when she was with us, all feeling somewhat guilty that we were glad she was going, but Mum heaved a sigh of relief.

CHAPTER
TWELVE

Not So Sweet Sixteen

Our years at Hayward School over, we were fast approaching our sixteenth birthday. It was a year of wildly fluctuating hormones which at times gave feelings of utter misery as we hovered between childhood and fast approaching adulthood. Neither of us were brimming over with self-confidence, and we were both still very shy. Every occasion brought with it the misery of trying to fit in and be one of the crowd. And of trying to overcome the feelings of inferiority instilled in us by the soul-destroying clashes with Mum and Dad, when we always seemed to lose credibility and become the butt of their many jokes. Anyone who has ever been shy will know the desperation of trying to merge into invisibility, and the horror of being noticed and brought to the fore. Never one to thrive on teachers' authority, my frantic efforts to remain in the background or a part of the scenery seemed to draw their efforts to pick me out, causing my face to flush brightly and hotly with a blotchy crimson. And squirming with embarrassment, I would fervently wish the very ground below my feet would open, to swallow me up, blotches and all. The pretty and confident girls in my class were now sneaking into school with makeup on, allegedly from the night before, and stiletto heels occasionally, to the wrath of the few teachers who took the trouble to notice. Still childlike and lacking a bosom, my appearance didn't help. I was spotty, rail-thin, with big feet clad in clumpy shoes that would have done a navvy proud. I was mousy and shy to boot. The dreadful tunic had now thankfully given way to a skirt, home-made by Mum in the dreadful woollen burgundy serge that she was afraid to wash regularly in case she had to replace it. It matched my face when the horrid bright red flush of nervousness crept up my neck as I battled with the ever-increasing blushes of sudden exposure to the teachers' efforts to draw me out. The sudden hotness and the prickly feeling in my neck and face, were sure signs that I had to make a bolt to the toilets and lock myself in until they cleared, or lose myself into my blouse as far as I could get.

Sex had reared its ugly head too. Overheard whispers in the toilets as I was "locked in" revealed who had done it with who last night. The fast set, usually the pretty girls, were deep into one-upmanship, and their latest liaisons featured heavily in a hot-bed of colourful gossip, passed round furtively and well giggled over by the awed and admiring few, who like me really hadn't a clue what they were talking about. The bike sheds near the playing fields were a haunt of the curious, eager to see if it really was all it was cracked up to be. There was one hullabaloo about a prefect who had them queuing up for his favours, which was eventually sussed by a curious teacher who followed the lines of twos and threes furtively wandering over to the playing fields after school, instead of to the bus stop to catch the bus home. After that the playing fields were placed out of bounds at dinnertime and after school, except for games of a more competitive nature, played after school and strictly supervised by a teacher. It was all over our innocent heads, however, and we dashed off home to snatch a cake from the shop window, despite the spots and huge mounds of homework in preparation for our forthcoming G.C.E.s. And then to watch the telly with a bag of sweets to keep the spots topped up.

Surprisingly there were no pregnancies at all among our contemporaries, which with hindsight makes me think it was all bragging, bravado and a lot of wishful thinking but no action. After all, it was just before the pill came out. No-one had to leave suddenly, and if they were like us there was no birth control knowledge passed on by Mum. As far as we were concerned, babies were found in the cabbage patch, or under the gooseberry bush if you had one. Since we didn't have either, there was no need to worry, and Mum didn't. But she kept an eye on the sanitary towels in the airing cupboard discreetly, just in case they were under the weeds in the back street as well. Some knowledge was passed on in biology. But we were all so embarrassed and flushed that not much sank in. The teacher wrote it on the blackboard, and did a few smudged drawings. Clearly he was as embarrassed as us because he had his back to us and never turned round, head either in the book he was copying from or nose an inch off the blackboard. He was a bit of a useless soul anyway, and his classes lacked discipline. By the time he had dodged all the dirty questions, and the whistles, and the bits of chalk thrown with catcalls at the mention of the words womb and phallus, the birds and bees were pretty well mixed up. He made a speedy exit, clearly relieved to have got the gist of it on the blackboard without having to turn round, in a fraught forty-five minutes of feigned deafness.

Pursuits of that kind were far from our thoughts anyway. It didn't matter. Far more pressing was the main thing on our mind. How to get Mum out of her clumpy shoe obsession which she was determined to pursue until the bitter end of our schooldays. In spite of it all, I do remember having a crush or two. One was on the young art teacher who caused quite a stir. Quite good-looking, and young, he was interesting and took time with us all, despite all the lack of talent in the class. We all swooned as he peered at the gunge of poster paint slapped liberally on to blue sugar paper, his hand on the back of our chairs, pointing out the artistic merits of the mess in front of him, head so close to ours we could smell the dandruff in his hair.

In spite of the secret crushes, neither of us managed to get a boyfriend until we were fixed up with a blind date at seventeen, by a friend. We managed to hang on to them for a while. I think they were more impressed with Mum and Dad's shop than by us. But they weren't too hard to shake off when Mum was counting the pennies and spreading the tea thinly so it didn't cost her any more. It soon gave them the full picture of Dad's wealth. Lois and Julia were going through the prefects at breakneck speed, but both managed to have steady boyfriends before we left school. Then again they had a head start on us of at least four years. We began to plaster the bedroom walls with pictures of 1950s pop stars. Yes, the word pop was coined in the 1950s. We started it all. Mum must have realised at last the fact that we were growing up, because after all the pestering she gave in to the high-heeled shoes. She was in the shoe club at Bearders, an old established shoe shop on Derby Street, paying sixpence or a shilling a week, whichever she could afford, until there was enough for a pair of shoes each. It was like Christmas had come. Mine were blue with pointed toes, in soft leather, which most shoes were made out of in those days. The heels were lower than I would have liked, but they were "high heels". Not enough to cut the mustard though with my school friends, who looked down with distain from their four-inch ones, twice the height of mine. They weren't pearlised either. Or the fashionable "oyster". So I was still out of step, so to speak; another blow to my status as I tottered about without much control on the two spikes, my toes all squashed in at the end. Dad likened me to Grandma Toothill, doing a take-off of us both tottering into the fireplace recess and back. By then I was past caring, and my feet were killing me. It was tough trying to be in the fashion, putting up with the shoes and being the butt of Dad's jokes.

Mum bought us some stockings to go with them as cotton socks just didn't look right. And suspender belts. Tights hadn't been invented then. The stockings seemed to finish just above the knees, with me being tall, leaving a gap between the stockings and suspenders that was hard to breach. And they were uncomfy. To top it all, they were rubber like the liberty bodice buttons, and went sticky and bendy, leaving red marks where they rubbed as I walked. Eventually the rubber bits perished, and the elastic went slack, leaving the stockings half up, or down, and a feeling of insecurity, because I didn't know when they would snap and drop off at some inopportune moment. Mum must have suffered for years, unknown to us all. Eventually, after a lot of moaning about them, Mum bought us a light control girdle each. A "roll on", which was better but still had the same rubber tabs on, even if they were higher and decreased the gap by stretching the stockings to such an extent that, with the control of the girdle and the stretched tension of the stockings, it was sometimes impossible to bend forward or down or anywhere. It did wonders for our posture, fearing a sharp "ping" at any movement and wondering if it was the suspenders or, even worse, the threaded knicker elastic that always went the same way. Were we thankful when tights appeared! They killed two birds with one stone and added a serene sense of security for ever, passion killers or not.

That last year at school Jean and I ended up in the same class. It caused some concern to our teachers, who couldn't tell us apart. Not that we thought we were that much alike any more, and we had very different personalities, Jean being more rebellious, and a scrapper like Mum with a quick temper at times. I was quieter, and more passive, like Dad, who would go to any lengths to keep the peace at home, especially with Mum, disappearing into the toilet when she came gunning for him and staying there until she had calmed down. Sometimes I wished I could join him, but there wasn't room for us both at once, so it was a race to get in first at any sign of trouble. Especially when her "nerves" started to play up later.

Jean had to start wearing glasses as well, which didn't please her very much either. But it was that or grope our way myopically to school. We often had rebellions about them, we hated them so much, and tried to do without them, but it was just no good. We were just too short-sighted to manage without. When Lois appeared in them one day, we couldn't help having a sneaky feeling of satisfaction, even if they disappeared into her school satchel most of the day. In spite of our insecurity about our looks, our trips to the CasaBlanca coffee bar increased, and most Saturday afternoons saw us perched on the high stools in the little dark front room after a morning looking at the shops. Clothes were becoming a bit of an interest, but Mum still insisted on taking us to C&A in Manchester for most of our clothes, usually one new outfit per season, her excuse being that we were in school uniform most of the week, which was true, I suppose. We dressed like mini-versions of Mum. The explosion of boutiques and their quirky clothing was still to come so we had no choice. Fashion for teenagers didn't exist. It was only in the 1960s that it really began to change with boutiques springing up all over.

Mum always had the last say, just like with the wallpaper for our room. We were often out-voted if she didn't think it suitable. Or if it was too expensive. We were allowed to choose the colour though so that was something. We did rebel, however, at being dressed alike, feeling it was childish at our age. We didn't have lots of clothes, either; Mum just didn't have the money, so every year we kept what fitted and added a Sunday best for good measure. We didn't know any difference, and most of our friends were the same. She made us dresses now and again, oddly gathered. In spite of all the sewing homework, she had slipped back into the quickly-does-it mode, and made it do. We always wore a cardigan over the top, anyway, so that covered most of the gathering oddities. Were we thankful when "the sack" came into fashion. There was no gathering to get right and Mum was delighted as they used less material, and seams hadn't to be matched up.

Derby Street was changing too. Some of the property had been knocked down and a huge block of flats was built on derelict land in Crook Street, much to Dad's delight as he acquired a whole lot of new customers. Some of the mills disappeared, too, and we noticed fewer clogs on the street, while the black shawls of our early childhood disappeared into memory. A change was coming but it was so gradual we didn't really notice it in the complicated business of growing up. A change of a different sort was coming to Mum. Now late into her forties, she was well into the menopause. As usual, Dad was the first recipient of her bad humour, being close at hand as the daily "dishing out" pervaded our home and Dad's bakehouse. The excuse given for her at times irrational behaviour was "nerves". Still being ignorant of the life cycle of women, we decided she was just plain bad-tempered and did our best to stay out of her way. Dad, sick of being on the receiving end, eventually packed her off to the doctor's, who said it was just her age and she should expect the fluctuations of her emotions along with the usual hot sweats and irregularities of her "on" days. It wasn't much comfort for us and Dad, who had to suffer the "nerves" at close hand as she mopped up the hot sweats and hit the roof at the slightest of things. There was much discussion in the shop as she whispered discreetly of her suffering and symptoms to fellow sufferers in the afternoon when the shop was slack, and the many remedies, all sworn to work, appeared on the kitchen windowsill the day after. Soon we were surrounded by Sanatogen products, and little liver pills, and Phyllosan, which was supposed to fortify the over-forties like Mum. They were all bought with high hopes and put in pride of place and near at hand. The various tonic wines which were recommended to "help with the symptoms" were hidden away in the back of the kitchenette, away from our curious fingers and the dodgy pull down worktop, which had a tendency to give way. All were to no avail; they had no effect. But they did keep her busy, dosing herself optimistically, much to our relief At the onset of her "nerves" we would all quickly disappear and leave her to it, hoping the tears and tantrums would subside before it was time for our tea. Poor Dad did his best to make her laugh in the forlorn hope she would forget her woes brought on by the attack of the "nerves" on her usually cheerful disposition.

All in all she didn't really get much sympathy as we hadn't a clue what she was suffering. Our sole aim was to dodge the bouts of her bad temper in the rush to school in the morning. One of the many things that riled her was the amount of time we spent preening in the kitchen mirror situated over the sink. Jean and I had acquired a bubble perm each at Ada Horrock's hairdressing salon on the next block down. It was all the latest fashion that year, with lots of bubbly curls all over our head, with a "kiss curl" either side of our forehead. Sometimes worn with a plastic headband, all the girls in our class had acquired the "look", and we were not to be outdone. It took a lot of persuasion when Mum was in one of her better moods but finally, to get a bit of peace, she gave in and coughed up the ten shillings each. Remembering Mum's attempts at perming, it was with some trepidation we entered the shop. We came back pink faced and curled up, relieved we hadn't suffered at Ada's hands quite as much as we had suffered at Mum's. We hot-footed it to school the next day after much patting and preening in front of the kitchen mirror, keen to be admired and as much in the fashion as everyone else. The look didn't last long, as the perm soon washed out and had to be re-curled with rollers overnight. They were murder to sleep in and dug into our heads, but, brainwashed into fashion-conscious ways, we put up with it. When the weather was wet, which it always was in Bolton, the curls dropped out straight away. It was very hard to keep it curled up, especially when the hair was naturally straight and wanted to stay that way. Mum got heartily sick of the dithering in front of the kitchen mirror and hogging the sink when she was trying to wash up. She must have sorely regretted that ten bobs' worth at Ada's which deprived her of her kitchen sink.

At school, our noses were kept firmly to the grindstone, and homework mostly consisted of going over what we had already learned. To be honest, not much had stuck in our memories but going over it brought it back and it proved to be tedious twice over. By the time the mock exams appeared, we were pretty well clued up and passed the exams easily, something which proved to be our undoing when the real exams arrived in the May and June of that year. Part of the exams clashed with Bolton holiday weeks, which upset Mum and Dad no end. Nothing could be done about it and, as it turned out, we only had two exams in the first week, so Mum and Dad managed to get away the second week after all. Exams apart, we managed to go out pretty often, neglecting homework and the boring revision to do so. The coffee bars were a great attraction and we always finished up in them instead of the reference library, where we were supposed to be revising away from the dinging bell of the shop.

When the fair came at New Year, we were drawn like magnets, teasing a bit of extra money from Dad for making the Christmas mince pies. We spent most of the money on the waltzers and dodgem cars, eyeing up the boys who worked on them at the same time, thinking they fancied us as they leapt on and off to swing the cars round. When Mum and Dad came with us at night, Dad always tried to win a coconut, and swearing they were stuck on when they didn't fall off the sawdust when he hit them. We always had to have one, so it was with finger crossed we stood watching the proceedings, until we could move on. Mum and Dad always enjoyed the fair. It was part of the Christmas festivity even when we grew up. Some of the stalls were a twist, especially the ball in a bucket. It was impossible to get one in, but it did keep the punters coming back. When Mum and Dad weren't with us, we would go into the "Naughty Nineties". Curiosity always got the better of us. It was like watching the brothel across the road. Naughty but nice, and very educational. The "girls" were always well past the flush of youth, but it didn't keep the young lads and dirty old men out. Or the curious like us. We stood with them all, necks straining to see the performance from the back where we thought we wouldn't be noticed. We were always disappointed too. There was usually nothing to see, because when there was the lights went out, leaving us still wondering why we had paid to come in when we could see Mum and each other for nothing.

The black peas always made up for it though, when we were cold enough. They were delicious, even if the hygiene wasn't up to scratch. There was nothing like a chipped cup of black peas on a frosty night, sitting in front of a blazing brazier on a hard bench seat with the wind whistling through the six inch gap under the tent and around your wellies. We always had to queue; they did a roaring trade despite the chipped cups. Sometimes we had two cups, which really isn't to be recommended because of the hygiene risk, and the after-effects of too much of the bicarbonate of soda they used to soften the peas. We never caught any harm, the after-effects being long over by the time we went back to school. Once we had thawed out we were expected to make room for other customers who were queuing after the same experience. If you hadn't thawed out after two cups, a third cup was really a no go area, and you had to pretend to look for the last black pea in the thick soupy mush and vinegar at the bottom of the chipped cup, poking out the very last pea with the battered old spoon, tasting of well-worn aluminium. Every so often the man in charge of the brazier jogged you along the bench, with a "Move up, please", and reminders to put the chipped cups in the big cauldron of lukewarm water to soak off the germs for the next customer. They would be fished out a few minutes later by a youth with dirty hands and put on a bit of dirty oilcloth for the next customer They don't taste half as good today. The hygiene has taken all the taste out of the experience.

After surviving the New Year Fair, it was back to school, swapping Mum's "nerves" for those of the teachers, who never seemed happy to see us. We were being bombarded by information from the school careers officer, who had been given the job of edging us out into jobs to keep us out of mischief, and to earn our keep until we could persuade some poor soul to marry us and perpetuate the species in a respectable way. Our ultimate goals in those days were to be Mums and housewives; there wasn't much ambition further than that, not for us anyway. Nurses, hairdressers, bank clerks, typists and shop assistants were what we aspired to and became in the gap between leaving school and marriage. Occasionally the top tier of the class went to teacher training college. That was posh in our part of the world, and as a northern accent wasn't really acceptable "down South", a few of our classmates had elocution lessons, to help them talk posh. They managed to get receptionists' jobs and the better jobs in posh shops, where it wasn't done to open your mouth and put your foot in it. Especially in a Lancashire accent.

Even when accents became popular with the Beatles, a Bolton one was still a cause for watching your Ps and Qs when going anywhere posh. When Dad was looking for staff it didn't matter to him. In fact, posh people made him decidedly uncomfortable, especially Mrs. Pike, who he took off to a T. Most of his staff were married women, part time. They often left when they got fed up with the early starts, so it was pretty on-going looking for bakehouse staff. Mum would put a card in the window with the hours, which put most of them off for a start. Only the hardy stuck it out, especially in winter when they were coming out in the dark early hours. Occasionally, when the card had put most people off, an advert was put in the *Bolton Evening News*, with a phone number, with Mum answering the phone in a business like voice to give the impression we were better than we were. They must have got a shock when they turned up and saw we were homely, and down to earth. Once she got carried away. Quite overtaken with the number of phone calls enquiring after the job, she got flummoxed and asked the poor applicant if she was experienced at both ends. Meaning shop and bakehouse. It was very hard for her to give any more details with us all rolling about laughing at the dirty connotations of her enquiry. In the end she had to change her knickers with the strain of it all. Needless to say, the poor woman didn't turn up to enquire further. She must have really wondered what the job entailed.

Some of Dad's staff brought their children during the school holidays, and we all amused one another in the back street, finishing up helping Dad to swill out and joining in our Pooh sticks in the sticky water in the gutter. Once we had grown up somewhat, the poor kids were left to amuse themselves. But most of them were well-behaved and well organised by their Mums who had to work to make ends meet. Some were very good and stayed for a while, and became friends who Mum and Dad were sorry to see go. Some were hopeless and had no feeling for the job. Dad couldn't wait to get rid of them, paying them a week's wage in lieu of notice because they were so useless. They had quite an assortment of people over the years, and all in all there was a lot of laughter among the hard work as these lovely characters came and went. Dad never made a fortune but he was happy in his work. It was only in the last few years of the job when he became unwell that he welcomed retirement with open arms. By then it had become difficult to compete with the vast number of supermarkets in the town so he called it a day, glad of the time to put his feet up for a while.

Our thoughts now turned to leaving school. Our childhood was at an end and it was time to move on. Most of the girls at school had jobs in the pipeline. Some had been going to typing and shorthand lessons on Saturday mornings at Lords Commercial College. They were well prepared for jobs in offices. It wasn't difficult to get a job in those days. You could walk out of one and get another one straight away. Jobs were plentiful in Bolton, and if you appeared bright at the interview, the job was yours. As the cotton mills closed down, they often provided office and warehouse space for a new type of business that was setting up in Bolton. Catalogue shopping was catching on fast, and a number of school friends acquired jobs at Brian Mills, which had just set up in the town. These were to become vast employment places in Bolton, Littlewoods and Great Universal Stores to name just a couple.

Dad wanted us to have a trade like he had, so I decided to try for a hairdressing apprenticeship. This I hoped would always provide me with employment, even after marriage and a family. Jean decided to try comptometer operating, which at the time was very well paid after training. She was enrolled in a school in Manchester to train. It didn't start until September, so she had the whole six-week holiday to herself. I had managed to get an apprenticeship at a hair salon in Walkden, nearby, and started the Tuesday after I left school. At the princely sum of thirty-one shillings and four pence, the wage just about covered my bus fare and dinner money. Mum was never going to be well off out of that, but we hoped it would get better. At least there wasn't a premium to pay. Some apprenticeships called for those, as much as twenty five pounds in some cases if it was a posh shop. Full of trepidation I caught the bus to my new grown-up world and was shown where to hang my coat. Mum had bought me an overall, which she had to provide, and it absolutely drowned me. If the worst came to the worst, it would give me a good place to hide. Paper nylon and lemon yellow, it hung on my gawky frame as I hovered shyly, not knowing what to expect. Confidence non-existent, face pink with the dreaded nervous flush it was impossible to conceal, I was taken in hand by another fellow apprentice and shown the ropes. Most of it consisted of washing towels, drying towels, folding towels and fetching towels. I seemed to be a mobile laundry. Busy as I was, I was glad the bulk of the work was in the back, out of the salon, giving my face, pink with the exertion and the heat of the laundering and the dreadful nervous flush, respite from the enquiries of "Are you all right, luv? You look very flushed" as I scurried back and forth loaded with wet towels, eyes glued to the floor in the hope of being left unnoticed. The morning stretched to weeks, and at last I was given leave of one hour to go for my "lunch". I spent it in the local chip shop, trying not to cry into my chips. I felt so lost and out of place. It was hardly the exciting world I had envisioned while still at school. They mustn't have known what to make of me either, because after an afternoon that lasted a month I was dispatched to catch the early bus home, no doubt so they could discuss my suitability.

Arriving home to enquiries of how it went produced floods of tears and all the pent up emotions of the occasion burst out. Mum and Dad were hardly sympathetic, either, and after the initial comforting to stem the tears, the humour of the occasion took over and they all had a good laugh at my expense. "You'll get used to it," was the cry, and I was packed off promptly at eight fifteen the following morning to make the best of it and earn my crust. Jean fared little better six weeks later when her time came to fly the nest. She also returned home in floods of tears, saying it was boring, she hated it, and the tutor was an ogre. She was also packed off sharp again the next day. After one week she refused to go again, saying she would never like the job even if it was well paid. Mum relented and she got a job in a shoe shop the following week, where she spent the next two years well-shod, happily selling shoes. The pay wasn't good and Mum stumped up for our keep. She never did make a profit out of us but Jean's staff discount helped buy all our shoes. As for me, well, I was taught the basics of hairdressing, cutting, colouring, and perming under the tutelage of a right old harridan of an employer. She overworked us all shamelessly, and ruled us with an iron rod for very little reward.

After ten months of the misery of it all, I rebelled, refusing to go again after a desperate cry for help and a walk half way to Preston to think things out. Mum stuck up for me, and tore her off a strip for the long hours she had made us all work. Quietly, they had been worried about the number of nights I was coming home on the last bus, standing at a bus stop late at night. They were always anxiously waiting as I got off the last bus. If I had missed it, it was a long five-mile walk after a fourteen-hour day. No wonder Mum and Dad were worried. She threatened to take me to court for breaking the apprenticeship contract, but a joint effort from Mum and Dad finally gave me my freedom, and a tongue-lashing from Mum finally finished her off. We never heard from her again, but she no doubt found another apprentice to exploit along the way. I later found a lovely lady to work for and we spent a happy ten years working together. She treated me like the daughter she had never had.

This journey through time to the very different world of my childhood has been both sad and happy, and somewhat illuminating as I have drawn on my memories of the past. The world I then knew in the 1940s and 1950s has gone forever. Some aspects of it I sorely miss, others not at all. There is no way back. Only in memory. The sense of community we shared with our near neighbours, when we all muddled through together, sharing humorous moments, was on reflection not a bad one. Most of these people who made up our childhood memories are gone now. They are a part of the past. After the world slowly changed in the 1960s and 1970s, I often wonder how they would have coped. The technology of the new age would have brought them an easier life but they were a hardy bunch, surviving two world wars with the little they were given. Their ingenuity was to be admired, and their temper, when they had little to laugh about, being generally cheerful and good-humoured. What little they had they were grateful for, and they never expected to be handed anything on a plate.

They weren't materialistic, there just wasn't the money, but they shared and borrowed what they didn't have from the neighbours, apart from money. They were too proud for that. For some, better times came, for others of course they never did. All in all life wasn't so bad, but along the way to prosperity I think we all lost something very precious. Maybe adversity brings out something special in all of us: an urge to protect the weak from the worst that life can throw at us. Our parents and Granny certainly protected us. We were a family unit, neither rich nor poor. We had a very ordinary childhood. Memory has a way of blotting out the bad things and perhaps if I tried harder I could recall a few, but this has been a happy journey of happy memories. The 1950s were certainly that. We never had it so good.

Perhaps my most enduring memory is of my father whistling as he swept and swilled out his bakehouse, while we played happily in our back street a game of Pooh sticks in the dirty water which ran down the gutter and pooled in a sticky mess around the grid in our cobbled back street.